PREVIOUS BOOKS IN SERIES

What If Jesus Was Serious?
A Visual Guide to the Teachings of Jesus We Love to Ignore

What If Jesus Was Serious about Prayer?
A Visual Guide to the Spiritual Practice Most of Us Get Wrong

What If Jesus Was Serious about the Church?
A Visual Guide to Becoming the Community Jesus Intended

What If Jesus Was Serious about Heaven?
A Visual Guide to Experiencing God's Kingdom among Us

A VISUAL GUIDE TO THE GOOD NEWS OF GOD'S JUDGMENT AND MERCY

WHAT IF JESUS WAS SERIOUS

ABOUT JUSTICE?

SKYE JETHANI

BrazosPress
a division of Baker Publishing Group
Grand Rapids, Michigan

Text and images © 2025 by Skye Jethani

Published by Brazos Press
a division of Baker Publishing Group
Grand Rapids, Michigan
BrazosPress.com

Printed in the United States of America

All rights reserved. No part of this publication may be reproduced, stored in a retrieval system, or transmitted in any form or by any means—for example, electronic, photocopy, recording—without the prior written permission of the publisher. The only exception is brief quotations in printed reviews.

Library of Congress Cataloging-in-Publication Data
Names: Jethani, Skye, 1976– author.
Title: What if Jesus was serious about justice? : a visual guide to the good news of God's judgment and mercy / Skye Jethani.
Description: Grand Rapids, Michigan : Brazos Press, a division of Baker Publishing Group, [2025] | Includes bibliographical references.
Identifiers: LCCN 2024031723 | ISBN 9781587436208 (paperback) | ISBN 9781493449828 (ebook)
Subjects: LCSH: Justice—Religious aspects—Christianity. | Jesus Christ—Teachings. | Mercy—Religious aspects—Christianity. | Christian life.
Classification: LCC BR115.J8 J47 2025 | DDC 261.8—dc23/eng/20240821
LC record available at https://lccn.loc.gov/2024031723

Scripture quotations are from the Holy Bible, New International Version®, NIV®. Copyright © 1973, 1978, 1984, 2011 by Biblica, Inc.® Used by permission of Zondervan. All rights reserved worldwide. www.zondervan.com. The "NIV" and "New International Version" are trademarks registered in the United States Patent and Trademark Office by Biblica, Inc.®

Scripture quotations labeled NLT are taken from the *Holy Bible*, New Living Translation, copyright © 1996, 2004, 2015 by Tyndale House Foundation. Used by permission of Tyndale House Publishers, Carol Stream, Illinois 60188. All rights reserved.

Scripture quotations labeled RSV are from the Revised Standard Version of the Bible, copyright © 1946, 1952, and 1971 National Council of the Churches of Christ in the United States of America. Used by permission. All rights reserved worldwide.

Italics appearing in Scripture quotations have been added by the author for emphasis.

Baker Publishing Group publications use paper produced from sustainable forestry practices and postconsumer waste whenever possible.

25 26 27 28 29 30 31   7 6 5 4 3 2 1

For Tim Johnson
"He has shown you, O mortal, what is good.
And what does the Lord require of you? To act justly and
to love mercy and to walk humbly with your God." (Micah 6:8)

CONTENTS

Introduction: Yes, and . . .   9

PART 1: Order *and* Chaos   19

PART 2: Horizontal *and* Vertical   67

PART 3: Judgment *and* Mercy   101

PART 4: Victory *and* Defeat   149

PART 5: Reward *and* Punishment   185

Notes   247

INTRODUCTION

YES, AND . . .

BACK IN 2010, Glenn Beck, the popular cable news political commentator, told his millions of viewers to "run as fast as you can" if your church ever talks about "social justice." Unfortunately, Beck never bothered to define what he meant by "social justice," except that it was a "perversion of the gospel" because, he argued, Jesus spoke about only individual compassion and not systemic evil.[1]

This kind of rhetoric has been commonplace within some streams of the American church for the last 150 years, and its origin is important for understanding the current shape of popular Christianity. So let's start with a brief journey through church history.

In the beginning, Christians understood their mission as having two dimensions rooted in the words of Jesus. When asked what the greatest commandment was, he said, "'Love the Lord your God with all your heart and with all your soul and with all your mind.' ... And the second is like it: 'Love your neighbor as yourself'" (Matt. 22:37, 39). This is why for centuries Christian mission involved both proclaiming the good news of peace with God through Jesus Christ (loving God) and the reformation of social evils (loving neighbors). And it is why the earliest Christians, as recorded in the book of Acts, cared for the poor, overcame barriers of race and class, and proclaimed the gospel to people outside the church. These dual values of personal faith and cultural transformation marked the church for generations and came to define what a Christian was.

For example, in the fourth century, a group of Christians brought food, water, and clothing to Egyptian prisoners. When one of the prisoners, a young peasant named Pachomius, asked who these caregivers were, he was told they were Christians.

"What's a Christian?" Pachomius asked.

"They are people who bear the name of Christ, the only begotten Son of God, and they are merciful to everyone, including strangers."[2]

The encounter transformed Pachomius's life. He later converted, was baptized, and became a leader of the church in North Africa.

This wedding of gospel proclamation (evangelism) and gospel demonstration (justice) continued to mark Christianity throughout

INTRODUCTION

the centuries, and individual acts of compassion transformed into movements of social reform. Christians invented hospitals and public schools, reformed prisons and the criminal justice system, abolished slavery, ended child labor, and advocated for women's suffrage. And these examples of neighborly love coexisted with the invitation to be reconciled to God, through Christ, and the forgiveness of sins.

But this two-dimensional mission began to change in the United States in the mid-nineteenth century. The country was deeply split over the issue of slavery. Abolitionists in the North argued that race-based chattel slavery was utterly incompatible with Christianity. Whites in the South, however, selectively read the Bible to argue precisely the opposite. In 1861, the Civil War erupted. Many pastors and churches, particularly in the border states, were eager to avoid a schism and somehow maintain their flocks.

That's when an upstart theological teaching recently imported from England exploded in popularity. It said the church's mission had only a single dimension—the saving of souls by proclaiming the forgiveness of sins through faith in Christ. And just as important, it said loving one's neighbors through the reformation of social evil was pointless. Departing from eighteen hundred years of Christian doctrine, this new theology said the world was racing toward imminent destruction and would be replaced. Therefore, reforming society was as pointless as polishing the brass on a sinking ship. All that mattered was urgently rescuing souls.[3]

INTRODUCTION

This new approach to Christianity gave white church leaders permission to ignore the debate over slavery altogether and, in some cases, to justify their own slave ownership. Likewise, after the Civil War, they could bypass other controversies about reconstruction, racial terrorism, segregation, industrialization, immigration, labor laws, and many other social and political problems. For large segments of the American church, Christianity morphed into an individualized faith about one's personal relationship with God, private morality, and escaping to heaven from an earth destined for destruction. In fact, in some segments of the American church, by the early twentieth century, any talk of reforming society or addressing systemic evil was shunned as outside the bounds of the gospel. Justice had become a betrayal of the true gospel.

Cue Glenn Beck.

Other churches, particularly in the North, recognized the mistake made by those who privatized and individualized Christianity, but as often happens, the attempt to correct one error resulted in another. Eager to embrace social activism and cultural relevancy, these churches began to downplay the importance of individual repentance, forgiveness, and salvation. Some even abandoned essential doctrines of the faith such as the deity of Jesus and his bodily resurrection. In their view, what mattered was fixing society, not saving souls.

For nearly two thousand years, Christianity had united loving God *and* loving neighbors. The church's mission was both inviting sinners to repent by giving their allegiance to Christ *and* influencing corrupt societies to reflect the values of God's kingdom more closely. But what God had joined together the modern American church put asunder. As a result, many in the United States have inherited a truncated understanding of the faith, with some Christians valuing justice but not evangelism and others valuing evangelism but not justice.

How do we heal this unnecessary and unbiblical division? I've found helpful tools from an unexpected source: improvised comedy.

A few years ago, I joined an improv comedy theater. I had no experience with improv or even theater, but after classes and coaching, I found myself drafted onto a performing team. Now I perform somewhat regularly. What separates improv from other forms of comedy, like stand-up or skits, is that it's completely unscripted. Everything is made up on the spot. This requires a unique set of skills that I did not naturally possess but slowly developed with time and practice.

The first and most essential tool of improv comedy is listening. Walking onto a stage with no script, no lines, and no plan is terrifying, and it's very easy to get lost in one's own head. *Who am I? What am I going to say? What will make people laugh? What should happen next?* This is a common and self-defeating problem. My coach, Jeff, would often tell me, "You've got to get out of your head so you can really listen to your scene partners." He was right. Their improvised decisions would inform my improvised decisions, and vice versa. But if I was focused on my own thoughts and ideas, I would miss the "gifts" they were giving me. "Gifts" are what Jeff called the oddball choices your scene partners make, and really listening is the only way to receive them and move the scene forward.

This is a lesson Christians divided over evangelism and justice can learn as well. The reduction of the church's mission to a single dimension—either social reform or saving souls—is most prevalent within modern, white, Protestant, American Christianity. But as already noted, it has not marked the historical church, and it's not true in most of the global church today. Even within the United States, most African American churches find no contradiction valuing both personal salvation and communal justice. These sisters and brothers have incredible gifts for any Christian seeking to understand the intersection of evangelism and justice if they would simply listen.

John Stott, an English priest and theologian, was a bit removed from the unique American context of slavery and racial segregation that led to the separation of justice from evangelism. As a result, his writing about the issue is incredibly illuminating. Expounding on Jesus's command to be both salt and light (Matt. 5:13–16), Stott states,

> We should never put our two vocations to be salt and light, our Christian social and evangelistic responsibilities, over against each other as if we had to choose between them. We should

INTRODUCTION

not exaggerate either, nor disparage either, at the expense of the other. Neither can be a substitute for the other. The world needs both. It is bad and needs salt; it is dark and needs light. Our Christian vocation is to be both. Jesus Christ said so, and that should be enough.[4]

I have witnessed white American church leaders and theologians argue and debate this issue ad nauseam, but for Stott and others outside the polarized American context, it simply isn't complicated or controversial. Jesus commands us to both preach the gospel and pursue justice. I've heard the same thing from Christian leaders in Asia, Africa, Europe, and Latin America. As one South African pastor said to me, "I just don't understand you Americans. Why is it so difficult for you to see that justice and justification belong together?"

That relates to the second tool of improv—"Yes, *and* . . ." When you are doing an improvised scene, your scene partner will invariably make an unexpected and bizarre decision. "Your job," my coach said, "is to say yes to that gift no matter what it is." For example, if your scene partner says, "Rover, you are the best dog in the world," then saying yes means getting on all fours and accepting the gift of being a dog. But it doesn't end there.

After accepting their choice by saying yes, it's your turn to add to the fun, the absurdity, and the emotion of the scene. This is where the "*and* . . ." comes in. The real joy of improv comes when

15

one choice is followed with an unexpected or incongruous choice that raises the stakes. A scene between the best dog and his adoring owner is fine, but a scene between the world's *best* dog and the world's *worst* dog owner—that's ripe for laughter.

Here's the point: tension builds energy. Tension is dynamic, compelling, and attractive. But so many debates in the American church over justice and evangelism ignore this truth and instead frame the issue as either/or. Rather than saying "Yes, *and* . . ." to all that Jesus said, too many assume that either justice or evangelism must take precedence over the other. This has led entire churches and denominations to say no to one gift of Christ's mission in favor of the other.

The testimony of Scripture, the words of Jesus, and the historical and global church, however, take a "Yes, *and* . . ." approach. They say yes to proclaiming the good news by inviting everyone into communion with God through Jesus Christ. *And* they mobilize believers to end oppression, seek justice, and cooperate with God to see his "will be done, on earth as it is in heaven" (Matt. 6:10). I believe we are called to embrace this life-giving tension as a gift and not reject it as a threat. And that is the approach I've taken in this book.

In part 1, "Order *and* Chaos," we will discover Jesus's definition of "justice" through the stories and laws of the Old Testament.

In part 2, "Horizontal *and* Vertical," we will see how our relationship with God can never be separated from our social relationships with others.

In part 3, "Judgment *and* Mercy," we will explore how both God's wrath and his forgiveness are rooted in love.

In part 4, "Victory *and* Defeat," we will examine the cross of Jesus as the moment of the world's greatest injustice and God's greatest triumph.

Finally, in part 5, "Reward *and* Punishment," we will discover what Jesus really said and did not say about judgment and hell.[5]

If you come from a Christian tradition that has minimized one aspect of Christ's mission in favor of another or that has flatly rejected justice as a betrayal of the gospel, I encourage you to not be distracted by the voices of tradition in your head. Only then will you be able to truly listen to the words of Jesus, the prophets, the apostles, and Christian sisters and brothers and discover gifts you didn't see before. Let's begin.

PART 1

ORDER *AND* CHAOS

LUKE 4:16-24

He went to Nazareth, where he had been brought up, and on the Sabbath day he went into the synagogue, as was his custom. He stood up to read, and the scroll of the prophet Isaiah was handed to him. Unrolling it, he found the place where it is written:

> "The Spirit of the Lord is on me,
>   because he has anointed me
>   to proclaim good news to the poor.
> He has sent me to proclaim freedom for the prisoners
>   and recovery of sight for the blind,
> to set the oppressed free,
>   to proclaim the year of the Lord's favor."

Then he rolled up the scroll, gave it back to the attendant and sat down. The eyes of everyone in the synagogue were fastened on him. He began by saying to them, "Today this scripture is fulfilled in your hearing."

All spoke well of him and were amazed at the gracious words that came from his lips. "Isn't this Joseph's son?" they asked.

Jesus said to them, "Surely you will quote this proverb to me: 'Physician, heal yourself!' And you will tell me, 'Do here in your hometown what we have heard that you did in Capernaum.'"

"Truly I tell you," he continued, "no prophet is accepted in his hometown."

1 IF JESUS WAS SERIOUS . . . THEN OUR UNDERSTANDING OF JUSTICE MUST BEGIN IN THE OLD TESTAMENT

TO BEGIN HIS PUBLIC MESSIANIC WORK, Jesus entered the synagogue in his hometown and read from the Hebrew Scriptures. He used the words of the prophet Isaiah to announce both his identity and his mission. This is not surprising given Jesus's Jewish heritage and that of his community. In a real way, everything about

Jesus's work, message, and ministry is built on the foundation of the Hebrew Bible. Therefore, we must start our exploration of justice where Jesus started: with the Old Testament.

As we've already noted, justice is a very popular subject today. It seems like everything, from economics to environmentalism, is now framed as a justice issue in our social discourse, but it's important to recognize that different definitions of "justice" exist, rooted in different traditions and assumptions. Just because two people both use the word "justice" doesn't guarantee they have the same thing in mind. It's a bit like being offered a slice of pizza. We should ask, "What *kind* of pizza? Neapolitan, Sicilian, Chicago style, New York style, Detroit style?" While these pizzas may share some traits in common, like having cheese or tomato sauce, the differences between a deep-dish pie from Chicago and a thin slice from New York are significant, and opinions about which is better are strongly held.

The same goes for justice. What a Marxist means by "justice" is very different from what a Mennonite means by it, and many political disagreements stem from divergent definitions of the word. So we must be clear about the distinctly biblical understanding of justice Jesus taught and practiced. It is revealed in the stories and poetry of the Hebrew Scriptures, and it's rooted in the character of Israel's God, which we will explore in this first part of the book. While Jesus's vision of justice may share some qualities with today's popular mainstream conceptions of justice, it is also distinct and must be understood within his own Jewish tradition.

ORDER AND CHAOS

To begin, two different but closely connected Hebrew words in the Old Testament are translated into English as "justice." One word is *tsedaqah*. It's a deeply relational and community-focused word that refers to the proper ordering of relationships. In the Hebrew tradition, a righteous or just person fulfills all of their relational obligations. Therefore, justice is not merely avoiding evil but faithfully living in relational harmony with God, others, and oneself.

The second Hebrew word for justice is *mishpat*. This word is used when relational obligations are broken and harmony must be restored. Timothy Keller says *mishpat* means "giving people what they are due, whether punishment or protection or care,"[1] so that each person and the entire community can flourish once again.

Unlike some modern concepts of justice that focus primarily on property, wealth, power, or individual identity, the biblical vision of justice—Jesus's vision of justice—is supremely *relational*. First, justice is about everyone in a community fulfilling their obligations to everyone else so that everyone can thrive together. Second, when these relationships become disordered, as they always do, biblical justice is the work of restoring order by righting wrongs. These themes of relationship, order, and restoration saturate the stories of the Old Testament that we must explore next.

 READ MORE: Psalm 33:4–5; Ezekiel 18:5–9

2 IF JESUS WAS SERIOUS ... THEN JUSTICE IS PART OF GOD'S CREATION

IN ANCIENT HEBREW, the words for "justice" are relational. They refer to the harmony that exists when things are in right order and in proper relationship to one another. And this is a distinguishing quality of Israel's God that we see in the opening verses of the Bible. In the creation narrative, we discover a God who delights in bringing order out of chaos.

Genesis 1 depicts the world as originally "formless and empty, [and] darkness was over the surface of the deep" (v. 2). Then God speaks and begins to separate darkness from light, sky from sea, and water from dry land. He begins to set the elements of the cosmos in their proper places, with boundaries and in harmony with one another, so that everything functions correctly.

Although we often want to read the Genesis story through our modern, more scientific point of view, to appreciate the emphasis of the Hebrew text, we must strive to read the creation narrative through the eyes of an ancient Israelite. That is what Old Testament scholar John Walton helps us do with his remarkable book *The Lost World of Genesis One*. After looking at other creation myths from Egypt and Babylon, Walton notes that these ancient peoples, like the Israelites, were not focused on the *material* origin of the world. In fact, "analysts of the ancient Near Eastern creation literature often observe that nothing material is actually made in these accounts."[1] Instead, the stories describe how the world is ordered to function correctly. For example, rather than asking "Where did the sun come from?" which is a material, scientific question, ancient peoples wanted to know "What is the sun's role in creation?" which is a story-oriented and relational question.

Walton goes on to describe the presence of three forces in the Genesis account. *Unorder* is the random, chaotic state of things before God acts. It's represented by the dark waters in Genesis 1:2. *Order* is the harmonious state created by God that brings wholeness and flourishing to all things. It's represented by the garden in Genesis 2. *Disorder* is the force that tries to tear down God's order

ORDER AND CHAOS

and return things to a state of chaos. Disorder is represented by the serpent in Genesis 3, where it schemes to corrupt the relationship between God and his creation.

Here's a simple analogy. LEGO sets begin as a chaotic pile of bricks (unorder), but they can be carefully assembled into, say, a tower, a house, or a truck (order) and then knocked down or crushed by a tyrannical toddler (disorder).

In the creation story, when everything is properly ordered, God calls it "good." This is what the Bible means by "justice"—everything is *just as it should be*. Evil, on the other hand, enters the scene when the serpent brings disorder to God's world by breaking the proper relationship between people and God, between the woman and the man, and between humans and the creation. To seek justice, therefore, is to cooperate with God against the state of unorder and the forces of disorder. Justice means joining with God in his creative and redemptive work to make things right again.

 READ MORE: Genesis 1:1–5; Isaiah 45:5–13

3 IF JESUS WAS SERIOUS . . . THEN ALL PEOPLE ARE MADE IN GOD'S IMAGE AND CRAVE JUSTICE

GIVEN THE PRESENCE OF JUSTICE at the beginning of creation, we should not be surprised to find justice at the center of every human civilization. Across a stunning diversity of beliefs, religions, philosophies, and cultures, people seem to agree on two things. First, this world is not what it ought to be, and second, we do not behave as we ought to behave. Both the Hindu and the humanist will lament when an earthquake razes a village or a disease kills a child. Likewise, both the believer and the atheist can agree that the powerful should not abuse the weak and the rich should not cheat the poor.

A sense of oughtness is universal to our species. As C. S. Lewis observes, "Whenever you find a man who says he does not believe in a real Right and Wrong, you will find the same man going back on this a moment later. He may break his promise to you, but if you try breaking one to him he will be complaining 'It's not fair' before you can say Jack Robinson."[1] While the particulars of what constitutes right and wrong vary somewhat across cultures, the categories themselves are universal. In other words, a vision of justice is innate to every human society.

A desire for a rightly ordered world, where things are as they ought to be, is shared by everyone. The only real division is between those who believe such a world is achievable and those who do not. One side says our craving for justice is the random product of evolutionary processes and that a sense of morality is nothing more than a chemical illusion of the brain to prevent our species from self-destructing long enough to pass our genes to a new generation. But the actual achievement of a fully just and ordered world is impossible. True justice is just a fairy tale.

The other side says we all carry a desire for justice because justice really exists and is actually achievable. No one argues that human desires for food, sex, companionship, and safety are mere evolutionary illusions designed to trick us into survival. We desire these things because food, sex, companionship, and safety *exist*. Why should justice be any different? We have physical cravings because we are physical creatures who occupy a physical universe. Likewise, we have moral cravings because we are also moral creatures who occupy a moral universe.

When the pursuit of justice is set aside as nonessential or a diversion from human flourishing—whether by unbelieving naturalists who say justice is an illusion or by religious fundamentalists who say justice is a distraction from more spiritual goals—the created order is contradicted. Our universal longing for justice shows that we humans are made in the image of a just God. While all people crave justice, Christians should be the very last people to deny or diminish its importance.

 READ MORE: Deuteronomy 32:1–4; Isaiah 56:1–2

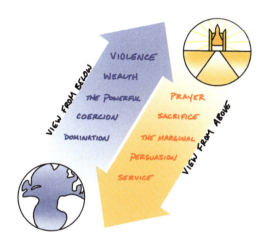

4 IF JESUS WAS SERIOUS . . . THEN EVIL EMPIRES WILL ALWAYS MISUNDERSTAND GOD'S JUSTICE

ABOUT SIXTY YEARS before Jesus was born, the Roman Empire invaded and conquered Israel. Jesus and his followers lived under the unjust occupation of a pagan empire their entire lives, but it was far from the first time God's people had experienced such conditions. In fact, the most important and foundational story in the Old Testament is about Israel's liberation from an evil empire. The story of Israel's exodus from slavery in Egypt profoundly shaped Jewish identity and imagination, as well as the Jews' understanding of God's justice. And Jesus used this story to interpret his own mission.

The story of the exodus begins with a dramatic change of circumstances for God's people. When the family of Jacob first arrived in Egypt centuries earlier, they were welcomed and they shared in the land's power and resources. A new king, however, did not view Jacob's descendants as valuable participants in his empire. Instead, he saw these immigrants as a threat to Egypt, so he persecuted and enslaved them. And to limit their influence, Pharaoh commanded "all his people" to throw Hebrew baby boys into the Nile (Exod. 1:22). The girls, however, were allowed to live. Apparently, Pharaoh did not consider women a threat to his empire, but using underestimated people to accomplish his purposes is one of God's specialties.

In the exodus story, it is women who repeatedly thwart Pharaoh's plans and become the subversive agents of God's justice. The Hebrew midwives refuse to kill the babies they deliver and then lie to Pharaoh when confronted. Moses's mother and sister scheme to evade Egypt's infanticide law, and it is Pharaoh's own daughter who rescues the infant Moses from her father's evil decree. The Lord uses these brave, overlooked women to subvert an evil empire.

Pharaoh could not recognize the subversive power of these women because in his vision of the world, they simply did not matter. They *couldn't* matter. His vision was from below; it was the vision of a worldly empire fueled by fear and built with coercion, domination, and injustice. He believed empires were ruled by kings, armies, and aggression. Therefore, he saw no value in slaves, women, and midwives.

The exodus story, however, reveals a vision of justice from above—from God's perspective. His way of using power turns things upside down. Victory comes through the forgotten and the marginalized, by abandoning coercive power and embracing subversive love. These themes, which are deeply rooted in the biblical narrative of God's people, are echoed by Jesus. He speaks of his kingdom spreading like yeast through dough or from a tiny mustard seed. In other words, his kingdom is subtle and often invisible rather than spectacular and obvious. And rather than affirming the powerful and the influential, Jesus gives his attention to children, women, the poor, and the sick—those ignored on the margins of society.

This was a counterintuitive message for Jesus's followers. Remember, they were living under Roman oppression, and many expected the Messiah to overthrow the pagan empire with spectacular force. The same temptation exists for us. Changes in our culture have some Christians frightened—particularly those who have benefited from the existing "empire." They

WHAT IF JESUS WAS SERIOUS ABOUT JUSTICE?

believe the God-given order of things is being threatened, and they're looking for leaders to restore how things used to be—even by force if necessary.

As with Pharaoh, however, fear causes us to misinterpret reality and ignore the nature of God's kingdom and justice. When we employ the world's vision of empire, we can be led to seek safety through leaders who *appear* powerful and aggressive and to dismiss the subversive influence of the meek and the marginal.

 READ MORE: Exodus 1:15–21; 1 Corinthians 1:18–25

5 IF JESUS WAS SERIOUS . . . THEN WE SHOULD RESIST EVIL

SOON AFTER GOD CREATED ORDER from the primordial chaos, agents of disorder appeared to corrupt his good creation. The serpent's scheme was wicked, but it became truly destructive when it found two willing accomplices in the garden: the man and the woman. Their cooperation with evil illustrates our universal human readiness to do wrong when the opportunity presents itself. But Scripture also shows people making the opposite choice by resisting evil.

In the exodus story, Pharaoh fears the growing strength of the Hebrews in his land. First, he tries to limit their influence by subjecting them to slavery. Denying them access to power, however, is not enough to alleviate his fears. Accordingly, he orders all male Hebrew babies to be executed at birth. The true fragility of empires is revealed in their tendency to view the most innocent and vulnerable as a threat and then target them for destruction. The story also shows how one man's paranoia created a national system of oppression against an entire community. The Egyptians willingly cooperate with Pharaoh's evil scheme against a less powerful minority.

But there is one unexpected group of subversives: the Hebrew midwives. Putting their faith in God rather than fearing the power of the empire, these brave women refused to obey Pharaoh's order to kill the newborn Hebrew boys, and when they were confronted by the authorities about their noncooperation, they simply lied. "Hebrew women are not like Egyptian women," they said. "They are vigorous and give birth before the midwives arrive" (Exod. 1:19).

The midwives' courageous defiance of Pharaoh's order reminds us of our call to stand against evil. Martin Luther King Jr. says, "Noncooperation with evil is as much a moral obligation as is cooperation with good."[1] I appreciate how Dallas Willard speaks about this aspect of the Christian life. He says we must practice "gentle noncooperation with evil."[2]

ORDER AND CHAOS

We see this same posture in the Gospels. While preparing the people for the arrival of Jesus and God's kingdom, John the Baptist courageously preaches a message of justice and noncooperation with evil. He tells those who collect taxes for the Roman Empire and often pocket the extra for themselves, "Don't collect any more than you are required to" (Luke 3:13). And he tells Roman soldiers not to abuse their authority. "Don't extort money and don't accuse people falsely—be content with your pay" (3:14).

Unlike some Jewish zealots, John was not advocating armed resistance to overthrow the Roman Empire. Instead, he called for gentle noncooperation with Rome's evil, trusting that ultimately God himself would bring permanent justice, as he did with Pharaoh and Egypt centuries earlier.

We may not all be called to lead great revolutions, but like the Hebrew midwives, we can gently subvert the evils we encounter every day. We can choose not to participate in gossip, we can stand alongside those who are persecuted, we can comfort those who are shamed for their nonconformity, and we can refuse to cheer the brutes or aid the bullies. If powerless midwives could find the strength to defy an empire, surely our Lord will give us the power to resist evil as well.

 READ MORE: Exodus 1:15–21; Luke 3:1–20

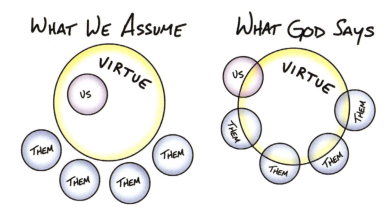

6 IF JESUS WAS SERIOUS . . . THEN GOD HEARS THE CRIES OF THE OPPRESSED

IN THE EXODUS STORY, the infant Moses is rescued from death in the Nile by an unexpected hero: Pharaoh's daughter. We are told that she "went down" to the river, where she "saw" the baby and took compassion on him when she heard him "crying" (Exod. 2:5–6). The words used to describe her maternal concern for Moses aren't particularly striking—until we get to the next chapter in the story.

In Exodus 3, the same words used to describe her care for Moses are applied to God's care for his people. The Lord declares that he has "come down" to deliver his people from their suffering. He has "heard them crying," and he has "seen" their misery (vv. 7–8). This very intentional linguistic link between Pharaoh's daughter and the Lord tells us two things.

First, although we often focus on God's fatherly attributes, his love also has maternal qualities. Just as a mother will not abandon her frightened and crying infant, neither will the Lord ignore the cries of his people. He will reach down, rescue, and comfort, just as a mother lifts and embraces her child. This is a strikingly intimate vision of God's justice within a story that often emphasizes his power and wrath. We see this same quality in Jesus when he approaches Jerusalem and says, "Jerusalem, Jerusalem, you who kill the prophets and stone those sent to you, how often I have longed to gather your children together, as a hen gathers her chicks under her wings, and you were not willing" (Matt. 23:37).

Second, linking the compassionate actions of Pharaoh's daughter with divine qualities shows the Hebrews did not have a monopoly on virtue. Throughout the Scriptures, the Lord frequently praises the righteousness of those *outside* the community of God's people. Just a few include Moses's father-in-law Jethro, Rehab the Canaanite prostitute, Naaman the Syrian soldier, and Ruth the Moabite. Beyond affirming the actions and faith of foreigners, some of these stories reveal the villain is actually an Israelite.

ORDER AND CHAOS

For example, Naaman comes to Israel seeking the prophet Elisha because he was told Israel's God could heal his leprosy. After having his skin restored "like that of a young boy" (2 Kings 5:14), Naaman offers Elisha an extravagant gift of gold, silver, and clothing. Elisha refuses, likely so Naaman will understand that Israel's God is not like pagan deities who expect compensation. While returning to Syria, however, Naaman is swindled by Elisha's servant Gehazi, who takes Naaman's wealth anyway. The story ends with Naaman, the foreigner, giving his allegiance to God, while Gehazi, the Israelite, is cursed and given Naaman's leprosy. The message of the story is important. Not all gentiles are wicked, not all Israelites are righteous, and the Lord sees beyond our group identity.

This strong biblical theme is a reminder that our human instinct to see those within our group (whether defined by religion, politics, nation, or ethnicity) as always "good" and those outside as universally "bad" is deeply flawed. Scripture reveals a far more complicated reality in which virtuous Egyptians (Pharaoh's daughter) and idolatrous Hebrews (like Aaron, who created the golden calf) exist. Faithful Syrians (Naaman) and wicked Israelites (Gehazi) exist. And this continues into the New Testament, where we find dishonest Christians (Ananias and Sapphira) and faithful pagans (the good Samaritan and the humble centurion). God's people do not have a monopoly on justice.

 READ MORE: Exodus 2:1–10; Matthew 8:5–10

7 IF JESUS WAS SERIOUS . . . THEN GOD CARES MORE ABOUT JUSTICE THAN IDENTITY

WE BEGAN THIS SECTION with the story of Jesus entering his hometown synagogue and reading from the scroll of Isaiah (Luke 4:16–24). He uses the Old Testament to announce his messianic identity and the nature of his mission to bring justice—the restoration of God's order. The people of Nazareth are understandably surprised and excited, but Jesus doesn't stop there.

He continues by referencing two more stories from the Old Testament. Both are about God's care for foreigners. During a famine, the prophet Elijah was sent to help a foreign widow rather than the many widows in Israel. And Elisha healed Naaman, a Syrian general with leprosy, but never a leper from among God's own people. After Jesus tells these stories, the vibe in the synagogue changes. "All the people in the synagogue were furious when they heard this" (Luke 4:28). In fact, they drive Jesus from the town and try to kill him.

Why the outrage? The Jews in Jesus's hometown, like people throughout the land at that time, were zealous about their Jewish identity. After all, they were God's chosen people. But they were living in humiliation under the oppression of a foreign, pagan empire. That's why they were so excited when Jesus read the prophetic words from Isaiah. The people expected the Messiah to arrive, defeat the Romans, and restore Israel's rightful place of glory above every other nation. Their patriotism swelled with hope.

Then Jesus bursts their bubble. The stories about the widow and the leper are about God giving preferential care to *foreigners*. In a not-so-subtle rebuke, Jesus is warning his neighbors not to give their primary allegiance to their ethnic or national identity but to put their hope in God. The people get the message and are furious. The idea that Israel's God would show kindness to pagans, to foreigners, and—heaven forbid—to *Romans* was shocking and insulting.

The error made by the people of Nazareth remains incredibly common today. It's all too easy to reduce God to a tribal deity, a small *g* god who fights for my team and no one else's, who is interested primarily in my group's flourishing and power. But a look back at the exodus story reveals a far larger vision of God's care and justice.

The descendants of Abraham suffered terrible injustice while slaves in Egypt, and in Exodus 3, the Lord declares, "I have indeed seen the misery of my people . . . [and] have heard them crying out. . . . I am concerned about their suffering. So I have come down to rescue them" (vv. 7–8). This is a remarkable revelation of God's compassion and pursuit of justice, but these verses also raise an important question: Does God act because the oppressed are *his people*, or does he act because his people are *oppressed*? In other words, does God respond because they are Israelites, to whom he has promised favor and protection, or does God respond because they are oppressed people made in his image? How does a person's identity affect God's response to injustice? It may seem like splitting hairs, but how we answer this question has implications for our understanding of God and his posture toward injustice.

If we put the emphasis on a person's identity, then God becomes a discriminating God who distributes blessing or punishment, justice or compassion based on which group we belong to. This is what the Jews in the synagogue in Nazareth believed—after all, God had shown his favor toward them throughout history—and it's why they were outraged when Jesus challenged the value of their Jewish identity.

Using a person's group identity as the basis for divine compassion can lead to the worst kinds of religious oppression, and we still see it at work. Much of our cultural discourse has deteriorated into feuds of tribal identity. *Those who belong to my religious/political/cultural group are favored by God, and those in other religious/political/cultural groups are not. In fact, those other groups are so wrong that they are unworthy of compassion.* Such thinking elevates identity above justice and may even cause us to excuse injustice perpetrated by those we think are favored by God.

If we keep reading in Exodus, however, we discover something remarkable. The Lord says to his people, "Do not mistreat or oppress a foreigner, for you were foreigners in Egypt. . . . If you do and they cry out to me, I will certainly hear their cry. My anger will be aroused" (22:21, 23–24).

The same language used in Exodus 3 to describe the Lord's compassion toward oppressed Israelites is used here to describe his compassion toward oppressed *non*-Israelites. Even more striking, just as the Lord unleashed his wrath on Pharaoh and Egypt for their unjust treatment of his people, the Lord now promises his wrath will burn *against his own people* if they abuse the foreigners in their land.

While teaching in the synagogue in Nazareth, Jesus echoes this part of the Old Testament law, a part his neighbors had perhaps

ORDER AND CHAOS

forgotten in their zeal. God hears the cries of the oppressed regardless of their identity, and his fierce wrath awaits their oppressors, whether they call themselves Egyptian, Roman, Israelite, or even Christian.

READ MORE: Exodus 22:21–24; Romans 2:6–11

WHEN YOU ARE HERE...

...DON'T FORGET WHEN YOU WERE HERE.

8 IF JESUS WAS SERIOUS... THEN EXPERIENCING OPPRESSION SHOULD GIVE US COMPASSION FOR OTHERS

WHILE IN EGYPT, God's people suffered terrible injustice. They were persecuted and enslaved by Pharaoh, who used them to build his cities and advance his empire. After the Lord rescued his people from the oppression of Egypt and gave them their own land, he commanded them to remember what they had endured and to never treat immigrants or foreigners unjustly.

Experiencing injustice ourselves should make us more just toward others, but history shows the opposite is often true.

Roger Williams was a Puritan who fled persecution in England for the New World. Along with other Christians who established the Massachusetts Bay Colony, he hoped to practice his faith without fear or political oppression. However, he was surprised to discover that the same injustice he had fled in England reemerged in Massachusetts within his own Puritan community. When he questioned a decision by the colony's rulers, he was banished to the wilderness. He survived only due to the kindness and mercy of Native Americans.

Based on his experience in both England and America, Williams became the first person to articulate the need for religious liberty and the separation of church authority from the civil state. He later established the colony of Rhode Island as a refuge for religious minorities, and his writings deeply influenced the founding generation of the United States. Williams argued that it isn't enough for persecuted religious minorities to separate and establish their own colony, because once they are at the helm of the ship of state, they quickly forget that they were once under the hatches. In other words, history shows that the persecuted can quickly become the persecutors once they have power.

We see this reversal in Scripture as well. Centuries after leaving Egypt, the Israelites become a powerful nation and begin to act like an empire. When Solomon becomes king, he builds great cities and palaces and, like Pharaoh, enslaves people to construct his empire. The Israelites are now at the helm, but they have forgotten what it was like to be under the hatches. Eventually, injustice toward the poor and immigrants becomes so rampant that God brings calamity on his own people, just as he had judged Egypt centuries before.

Some Israelites of this period excused their injustice because of their special identity. They assumed God had judged Egypt *because* they were Egypt and God had blessed Israel *because* they were Israel. In other words, they believed identity was more important than justice and that their status as God's covenant people exempted them from the kind of punishment Egypt had experienced.

In fact, they had things backward. It was precisely *because* they were God's covenant people, *because* they had known injustice themselves as slaves, *because* God had rescued them with his mighty hand and outstretched arm, and *because* they had been given God's commands to show kindness to foreigners that he judged them so severely. In short, of all people, the Israelites should have known better.

The same can happen to us if we lose sight of what Christ has rescued us from. We can easily stand in judgment over others or carry a sense of self-righteous superiority rather than show compassion and kindness to others. This happens when we lose sight of our own hopelessness apart from God. We may even be

WHAT IF JESUS WAS SERIOUS ABOUT JUSTICE?

tempted to hide behind our identity as Christians to justify our mistreatment or hatred of others, all the while priding ourselves for standing against evil. The truly righteous person remembers their own sin. As a result, they respond to the sin of others with greater compassion rather than greater judgment. Living justly means never forgetting what it was like to live under the hatches, even when we find ourselves at the helm.

 READ MORE: Deuteronomy 24:17–22; Matthew 18:23–35

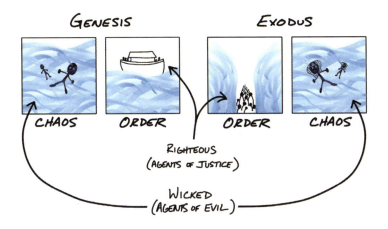

9 IF JESUS WAS SERIOUS... THEN EVIL WILL CONSUME THOSE WHO PRACTICE IT

IN THE BEGINNING, the world was unordered and disorganized. This state of chaos is represented by the dark waters of the abyss in Genesis's creation narrative. But we read that God's Spirit hovered over the sea and separated the waters to create the sky, then gathered the sea in one place to create dry land. God set boundaries, contained chaos, and put all things in their proper relationship with one another so that life could flourish.

As we will see, this theme is not limited to the creation story. The contrast between God and the sea, between order and chaos, between justice and evil continues all the way through the Bible. In Genesis 6, we learn that violence and corruption consume all the people. Grieved by the evil he sees, the Lord allows the chaotic waters to return and cover the world. Those who practice disorder and injustice, those who refuse to participate in God's ordering of creation, are given over to the chaos of uncreation. They are taken by the flood—the primordial waters that represent disorder and evil—but God protects Noah and his family through the deluge.

This same theme is repeated in the exodus story. The Lord has rescued his people from oppression and slavery in Egypt, but Pharaoh's army pursues them and traps them along the sea. But like he did in the beginning, God separates the waters. He brings order from chaos and rescues his people by bringing them through the sea on dry ground. And when the Egyptians follow them, we are told that "the water flowed back and covered the chariots and horsemen—the entire army of Pharaoh that had followed the Israelites into the sea. Not one of them survived" (Exod. 14:28). As with Noah's flood, the injustice and evil of Egypt are consumed by raging waters.

Two important ideas are established in these foundational biblical stories. First, God creates order from disorder so that his people—and all of creation—can flourish. This God-ordained order is what we call justice. It's the life-giving order that exists when

ORDER AND CHAOS

everything is in its intended place and everyone lives in right relationship with God and one another.

Second, these stories reveal the fate of those who practice and perpetuate injustice, who reject God's order to pursue evil and oppression. Rather than reflecting the image of the Creator, who brings justice and flourishing, they become children of chaos, and chaos eventually consumes them. Ultimately, they are overwhelmed by the waters and washed away.

 READ MORE: Exodus 14:15–31; Mark 4:35–41

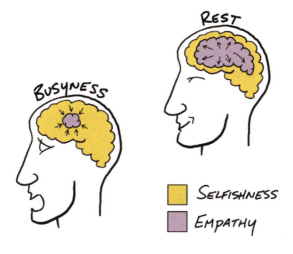

10. IF JESUS WAS SERIOUS... THEN REST IS HOW WE REMEMBER AND EXTEND JUSTICE

WHEN JESUS ENTERED THE SYNAGOGUE in his hometown and read from the scroll of Isaiah, the passage he chose was about "the year of the Lord's favor," or what the Old Testament calls the Year of Jubilee (Luke 4:19; Isa. 61:2). To understand the Year of Jubilee, we must first recognize the way time was ordered in ancient Israel.

In the Old Testament, the Lord commands his people to rest from all their work on the seventh day of every week. The reason for this day of rest, known as the Sabbath, is given in Deuteronomy 5. The Lord says, "Remember that you were slaves in Egypt and that the LORD your God brought you out of there with a mighty hand and an outstretched arm. Therefore the LORD your God has commanded you to observe the Sabbath day" (v. 15). In other words, a day without labor—which they never got while enslaved in Egypt—was meant to remind the Israelites that God had set them free. His justice had prevailed.

But the Sabbath went even further. Every seven years, Israel was to let the land rest for one year. They were not to plant or harvest but instead allow the soil to rest and replenish its nutrients.

Finally, after seven cycles of seven years (or forty-nine years), the fiftieth year was designated a year of jubilee, or "the year of the Lord's favor." In that year, all property that had been bought and sold during the previous forty-nine years was to be returned to its original owners, and all debts were to be forgiven. In a way, the Year of Jubilee was like hitting the economic reset button on Israelite society. It ensured that cycles of generational poverty would be broken and that the systemic oppression the people had experienced in Egypt would not be repeated in their own land.

Whether resting from work every seventh day or forgiving debts every seven times seventh year, Sabbath was inexorably connected to justice. God wanted the personal and corporate lives of his people ordered in a way that prevented oppression and encouraged everyone's flourishing. That's what makes the way many Christians practice the Sabbath today so strange. In many Christian communities, Sabbath has been reduced to a discipline of personal piety rather than one of social concern. Jesus did not make this error. That is why he often healed people on the Sabbath—and provoked the ire of religious leaders in the process. Jesus recognized that Sabbath was about more than not working. It was about freedom, liberation, and justice. Therefore, freeing people from the oppression of sickness, blindness, paralysis, and evil powers was part of his Sabbath observance. That means our Sabbath practices can also include serving the poor, caring for the sick, and alleviating the burdens that imprison others.

Remember, in the Old Testament, the Lord tells his people to rest on the seventh day for two reasons. First, to remember how he delivered them from slavery. And second, so that they can extend that same rest to others—especially those at the very bottom of the social hierarchy, including servants, immigrants, and even animals (see Deut. 5:14). And when Israel failed to use the Sabbath in this way, when they made the day into one of personal prayer and worship that ignored the poor, overlooked the oppressed, and mistreated workers, God rejected their prayers and songs (see Isa. 58:1–14).

These two elements of the Sabbath—remembering God's justice in the past and empathizing with the oppressed today—are both made possible when we slow down and rest. A 2013 neuroscience study found that self-centeredness, not empathy, is the default setting for the human brain.[1] This selfishness, however, is kept in check by a part of the brain called the right supramarginal gyrus. It helps us recognize the emotions of others and respond with empathy and compassion. There's just one problem. The brain's empathy center (the right supramarginal gyrus) functions much slower than the selfish parts of the brain, and researchers have found that when we are distracted or make rapid decisions, empathy is dramatically reduced.

Cultivating empathy, therefore, requires slowing down enough for reflection, self-awareness, listening, and focused attention, and these things are possible only when we rest from our work. In other words, practicing the Sabbath gives us space to remember God's justice *and* equips us with the empathy necessary to extend his justice to others the way Jesus did.

Today's hyperactive, noisy, digital environment seems devilishly designed to shut down the brain's empathy center. Social media provokes us to react rather than reflect, and even many worship settings are designed to flood us with external stimulation rather than foster inward connection. Is it any wonder our society is becoming more fearful, angry, polarized, and incapable of compromise? If we really want to awaken empathy, grow in godliness, and establish a more just and compassionate world, we need to start by unplugging and slowing down. We need to begin with practicing the Sabbath.

 READ MORE: Leviticus 25:8–18; Isaiah 58:1–14

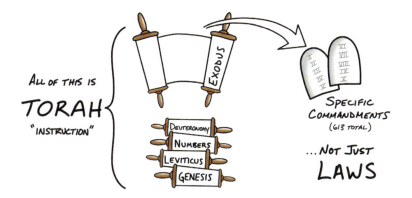

11 IF JESUS WAS SERIOUS... THEN JUST LAWS WILL LEAD TO COMMUNITY FLOURISHING

AFTER SEPARATING THE WATERS OF THE SEA, rescuing his people from slavery in Egypt, and destroying Pharaoh's army, the Lord leads the Israelites into the wilderness to Mount Sinai. God's own presence descends on the mountain, where he meets with Moses. Popular culture remembers this as the scene where Moses receives the Ten Commandments. That is true, but the Lord gives him much more than just two stone tablets.

63

Sinai is where God establishes his covenant with Israel, his special relationship with the descendants of Abraham. The Ten Commandments are part of this relationship, but the Lord actually gives the people hundreds of laws that cover a wide spectrum of topics, from dietary restrictions and sexual ethics to economic policies and judicial guidelines, even to architectural plans and procedures for worship gatherings. Taken together, the revelation of God and these commands given to Moses at Sinai are known as the *Torah*, a Hebrew word meaning "instruction," sometimes translated "the law."

Some mistakenly limit the Torah to the 613 specific commands given to Israel. In fact, the Israelites defined the first five books of the Bible in their entirety as "the Torah." (These books are sometimes called the books or scrolls of Moses, and they include Genesis, Exodus, Leviticus, Numbers, and Deuteronomy.) They include many commandments but also many stories, including the creation account, the flood, the stories of Israel's patriarchs (Abraham, Isaac, and Jacob), the accounts of Moses, the deliverance from slavery in Egypt, and many more. By identifying both direct commandments and these narratives as Torah, the people understood that both were instructive. Both were to shape and order how God's people lived.

Many contemporary Bible readers haven't been taught to see the link between the exciting stories contained in the Torah and the less thrilling chapters of archaic laws. The flood in Genesis is a riveting tale. But what about the list of purification rituals required for various skin diseases in Leviticus? Not so much. We usually skip these chapters because we view them as a distraction from the main flow of the Bible. But they're not.

Remember, from the opening verses of Genesis, God has been cultivating justice. He has been creating order from unorder and putting things in proper relationship so that life can flourish. This is what the creation story, the flood, and even the rescue from slavery in Egypt are all about. At Mount Sinai, this same divine work continues, but in a new way. The instructions given to Moses are God's way of properly ordering his relationship with Israel, and they are wise guidelines for how the ancient Israelites should properly relate to one another so that everyone can experience life and blessing. In this way, the entire Torah—including both the stories and the commandments—is about rightly ordered relationships. In other words, the Torah is all about justice.

This theme emerges in the New Testament as well. The Gospel of Matthew, in particular, is structured to mimic the Torah. Just as the Torah contains five books, Matthew's Gospel is written in five parts, each one ending with the phrase "after Jesus had finished instructing," "when Jesus had finished saying these things," and the like (see Matt. 7:28; 11:1; 13:53; 19:1; 26:1). The Hebrew word *torah*, as already noted, means "instruction." And just as Moses ascended Mount Sinai to receive God's instructions, the first section of Matthew's Gospel depicts Jesus giving his instructions

WHAT IF JESUS WAS SERIOUS ABOUT JUSTICE?

in a sermon on a mountain.[1] This is why N. T. Wright says, "One of the main things Matthew wants to tell us is that Jesus is like Moses—only more so."[2]

Just as the Torah cares deeply about order and justice, so does Jesus—only more so. Rather than merely giving us external commands to rightly order our relationships with God and others, Jesus is interested in a deeper kind of order. And that is what we will explore next.

 READ MORE: Matthew 5:17–20; 7:15–20

PART 2

HORIZONTAL *AND* VERTICAL

MATTHEW 5:21-24; 6:14-15

You have heard that it was said to the people long ago, "You shall not murder, and anyone who murders will be subject to judgment." But I tell you that anyone who is angry with a brother or sister will be subject to judgment. Again, anyone who says to a brother or sister, "Raca," is answerable to the court. And anyone who says, "You fool!" will be in danger of the fire of hell.

Therefore, if you are offering your gift at the altar and there remember that your brother or sister has something against you, leave your gift there in front of the altar. First go and be reconciled to them; then come and offer your gift. . . .

For if you forgive other people when they sin against you, your heavenly Father will also forgive you. But if you do not forgive others their sins, your Father will not forgive your sins.

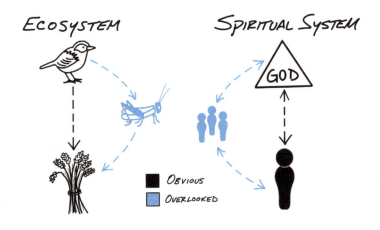

12. IF JESUS WAS SERIOUS... THEN JUSTICE MUST PERMEATE OUR RELATIONSHIP WITH GOD AND OTHERS

IN 1958, the Chinese government began a nationwide campaign to rid its country of sparrows. The small birds, the government claimed, were responsible for eating grain that was needed to feed the country's growing population. Millions of citizens were mobilized to trap and kill the birds, destroy their nests, and crush their eggs. The campaign was effective. By 1960, the birds had been virtually eradicated from China.

That was also when the government realized sparrows do not eat grain only; they also eat insects. With their predators gone, insects multiplied, and more rice was lost to pests than before the anti-sparrow campaign began. The ecological imbalance contributed to a famine that killed an estimated 45 million people. Eventually, China replenished its sparrows by importing 250,000 birds from the Soviet Union.

We know from the natural sciences that ecosystems are complex webs of interdependence. A small change in one part can greatly affect another part. It is very difficult—and usually very unnatural—to isolate a single variable in an interconnected network. This is true not only of ecosystems but also of economic systems, social systems, and even spiritual systems. Unfortunately, like the Chinese government, we, too, often compartmentalize and fail to recognize how seemingly unrelated things may actually be connected. This lack of imagination can have tragic consequences.

For example, the Old Testament repeatedly identifies a connection between Israel's relationship with God and its relationships with one another. Failing to act justly toward orphans, widows, immigrants, and the poor, the Lord says, will result in a broken relationship with him. He vows to reject Israel's prayers and worship and even expel them from the land. In a sense, God expects justice to permeate the spiritual ecosystem of Israel; injustice in one part ultimately reverberates through every part.

Given the dominance of this theme in both the Torah and the Prophets of the Old Testament, we shouldn't be surprised that Jesus frequently emphasizes it as well. In his Sermon on the Mount, Jesus teaches that the way we treat others will determine how our heavenly Father treats us. For example, he says, "Blessed are the merciful, for they will be shown mercy" (Matt. 5:7). He warns us to reconcile with our brother or sister *before* we worship God (5:23–24). And Jesus makes it clear that God's forgiveness must not be separated from our call to forgive others (6:14–15).

Perhaps the reason we find this theme throughout Scripture is because the Lord knows our human inclination to segregate and isolate justice. We desperately want to believe we can have a rightly ordered relationship with God while simultaneously despising, mistreating, condemning, and violating the dignity of those created in his image. This is one of the most common and destructive delusions within religious communities. In fact, when religious people lose sight of the interconnected reality of justice, it's not uncommon for them to use their relationship with God to justify their mistreatment of others.

 READ MORE: Isaiah 58:1–14; 1 John 4:7–21

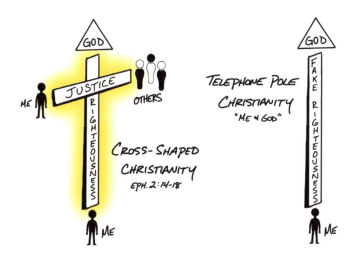

13. IF JESUS WAS SERIOUS... THEN OUR WORSHIP OF GOD WILL BE MULTIDIMENSIONAL

JESUS HAD A REPUTATION for healing on the Sabbath. The religious leaders saw such healing as a violation of the Torah, which forbade work on the seventh day, and definitive proof that Jesus could not be a true prophet, let alone the Messiah. God's chosen Savior, after all, would not disregard God's own laws. Such a reality may have been why a Pharisee invited Jesus to his home on the Sabbath for a meal. Luke tells us that Jesus "was being carefully watched" when a very ill man came before him (Luke 14:1–2). The whole scene feels like a setup. They have been trying to catch Jesus breaking the law, but he deftly turns the trap on them.

Jesus asks, "If one of you has a child or an ox that falls into a well on the Sabbath day, will you not immediately pull it out?" (Luke 14:5). Recognizing the trap, the religious leaders don't answer. Jesus proceeds to miraculously heal the sick man as the self-righteous dinner guests remain silent.

Why don't they answer Jesus's question? And why don't they object to his "work" of healing on the Sabbath? Because they know the Torah makes an exception on the Sabbath if someone's life is in danger. In Jesus's scenario of a son or an ox falling into a well, death is not an immediate risk, but the Pharisees know they would each pull them out in violation of their own strict reading of the law. In other words, Jesus is showing his hosts that none of God's laws forbid compassion. In fact, our devotion to God should promote, never prevent, merciful actions toward those in great need. The real sin is not healing on the Sabbath but failing to recognize the inherent value of a person burdened by illness.

True religion will never allow the first part of the great commandment ("Love the Lord your God with all your heart...") to become an excuse for not obeying the second part ("Love your neighbor as yourself"). Religious people throughout the ages have tried to separate the two. Yet throughout both the Old and the New Testaments, the Lord makes it abundantly clear that the primary way we honor, serve, and worship him is by loving, serving, and honoring those created in his image. For example, in the book of Isaiah, God's people are engaged in religious rituals of worship, including fasting, to express their deep devotion to the Lord, but he utterly rejects these religious activities. Why? Because their worship of God does not translate into compassion and justice toward the poor and the oppressed (see Isa. 58).

Columnist David French calls this narrow focus on religious devotion "telephone-pole Christianity." People who focus only on their vertical relationship with God, French says, are like telephone poles—they are one dimensional and "siloed in this personal relationship with Jesus." But we are called to a two-dimensional faith, wherein two poles intersect to form a cross-shaped Christianity and our vertical connection to God supports and empowers our horizontal engagement with our neighbors. In French's view, that means engaging the call of the gospel to "ameliorate injustice in the world."[1]

It's a simple but useful metaphor that also explains the core conflict between Jesus and the religious leaders. The devout, self-righteous dinner guests in Luke's story practice a telephone-pole faith in which the Sabbath is about honoring God and nothing more. Jesus, however, represents a cross-shaped faith in which his devotion to the Father is *always* revealed through his love and compassion for others. Therefore, Jesus's act of healing a suffering man is a way of worshiping God on the Sabbath. We shouldn't be surprised today when those who insist on uniting their Christian faith with justice and compassion are accused, like Jesus was, of being unfaithful to God's law.

Telephone poles dot today's religious landscape—but it's the cross that heals the world.

READ MORE: Isaiah 58:1–14; Luke 14:1–14

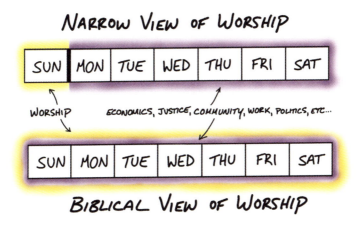

14. IF JESUS WAS SERIOUS . . . THEN JUSTICE IS ESSENTIAL TO WORSHIP

MANY OF US HAVE BEEN SHAPED to think of worship as synonymous with music. In fact, we often label the musical part of a church gathering as "worship" and distinguish it from prayer, Scripture reading, the sermon, or communion. I will confess that when I hear people use "worship" as a synonym for "music," it annoys me both as a student of the Bible and as someone who is musically impaired. We have so narrowed the definition of worship that we cannot even recognize that many nonmusical activities can also bring praise and glory to God.

In Scripture, worship is far broader than music or singing. In fact, it transcends even creativity or artistic expressions of devotion. Worship is not merely what God's people do in large religious gatherings. Some are surprised to discover that both the Old and the New Testaments deeply connect the act of worship to economic and communal justice.

In his book *The Dangerous Act of Worship: Living God's Call to Justice*, former Fuller Seminary president Mark Labberton writes,

> According to the narrative of Scripture, the very heart of how we show and distinguish true worship from false worship is apparent in how we respond to the poor, the oppressed, the neglected and the forgotten. As of now, I do not see this theme troubling the waters of worship in the American church. But justice and mercy are not add-ons to worship, nor are they consequences of worship. Justice and mercy are intrinsic to God and therefore to the worship of God.[1]

Labberton goes on to show that our pursuit of justice Monday through Saturday cannot be separated from what we do when we gather on Sunday. He also shows why our commitment to justice may determine whether God accepts or rejects our praises and prayers. Such realities represent a serious challenge to our compartmentalized view of faith. We have been shaped by a culture of hyperindividualism and a modern Christian tradition that emphasizes one's "personal relationship with God." This culture and this tradition lead us to see worship and other dimensions of our spiritual lives as hermetically sealed off from our social, cultural, political, and economic life. Faith is something we engage privately, and worship is merely between my heart and God—even when I'm singing alongside hundreds of others.

This narrow definition of worship and this individualized vision of faith are why seemingly devout Christians can mistreat their employees, show indifference toward a suffering group they do not identify with, or support policies that exploit the poor—and still lift their hands to praise Jesus with enthusiasm on Sunday. They assume these parts of their life exist in distinct, isolated spheres. But they do not.

Consider how you have been taught to think about worship. Do you associate it primarily with music? Is worship merely what happens during a church gathering and primarily about how you emotionally connect with God? Or were you given a vision of worship that extends to every part of life and every person you encounter? If so, how does worship shape your pursuit of justice?

 READ MORE: Isaiah 1:10–17; 1 John 4:19–21

Consumer Christianity's Worship Evaluation
My church's worship helps me FEEL...
- [ ] ENTERTAINED
- [ ] EXCITED
- [ ] INFORMED
- [ ] LOVED
- [ ] COMFORTED
- [ ] INSPIRED

Jesus Christ's Worship Evaluation
My church's worship helps me BECOME...
- [ ] JUST
- [ ] COMPASSIONATE
- [ ] MERCIFUL
- [ ] LOVING
- [ ] GENEROUS
- [ ] HUMBLE

15 IF JESUS WAS SERIOUS... THEN TRUE WORSHIP LIFTS UP CHRIST BY LIFTING UP THE OPPRESSED

EVERYONE SEEMS TO HAVE AN OPINION about worship. Traditional or contemporary? Band or choir? Hymns or choruses? Upbeat or contemplative? Sometimes, divergent tastes can split a congregation. And for an increasing number of people, the musical performance on Sunday—which is how many have come to define the word "worship"—is *the* critical factor in choosing a church home. Rick Warren, one of the most influential pastors in the country, has noted, "Music may be the most influential factor in determining who your church reaches for Christ, and whether or not your church grows."[1]

But what does God look for in our worship? After all, the church's worship is supposed to be for *him*. Right?

Isaiah 58 gives us a surprising glimpse into what matters to God. The Israelites have devoted themselves to ritual worship and acts of piety to express their humility before the Lord. Such worship and piety include fasting, bowing low to the ground, wearing sackcloth and ashes, and offering prayers and sacrifices. These are the ancient equivalents of sacrificing our leisure time on Sunday mornings, participating in enthusiastic singing, and giving our time and treasure to the church's ministries.

But in Isaiah 58, the Lord utterly rejects the worship of his people because they have made it into an act of personal piety rather than one of communal justice. Their worship is inward and disconnected from the needs of those around them. The Lord says:

> Is not this the kind of fasting I have chosen:
> to loose the chains of injustice
>   and untie the cords of the yoke,
> to set the oppressed free
>   and break every yoke?

HORIZONTAL AND VERTICAL

> Is it not to share your food with the hungry
> > and to provide the poor wanderer with shelter—
> when you see the naked, to clothe them,
> > and not to turn away from your own flesh and blood?
> (vv. 6–7)

The question we should focus on to evaluate our worship is not whether we like the music or even whether the order of the service follows some biblical formula but whether our worship moves us to love and serve the oppressed. Does it inspire us toward compassion, mercy, and justice for the poor? False worship, no matter the style, is always marked by an inward, narcissistic posture of personal piety that is severed from the realities of the world. False worship will always insist that what we do in a church service matters more to God than how we act toward our neighbor, the stranger, or our enemy—the opposite of what Jesus teaches when he commands us to pursue relational reconciliation before religious rituals (see Matt. 5:23–24).

True worship, on the other hand, will shape us into the image of our God, who entered into the brokenness of the world to rescue, heal, and redeem. It will form us as true disciples of Jesus and restore our original human vocation to be God's representatives in every part of creation. The particular style of music or liturgy isn't nearly as important as how our worship inspires us to see and act in the world. So the next time you evaluate the worship of your church, rather than judging the excellence of the music or the beauty of the liturgy, ask what the congregation is doing to alleviate the suffering of those in the wider community. True worship means lifting up the name of Christ by lifting up the oppressed.

 READ MORE: Isaiah 58:1–15; James 2:14–24

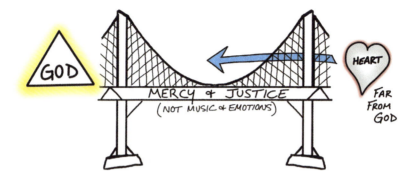

16. IF JESUS WAS SERIOUS . . . THEN A HEART FAR FROM GOD LACKS MERCY, NOT EMOTIONS

POPULAR CULTURE CARICATURES the God of the Old Testament as wrathful and petulant, demanding animal sacrifices and issuing arbitrary commandments. The Jesus we encounter in the New Testament is often caricatured as merciful, indifferent about rituals, and socially inclusive. These caricatures bifurcate the persons of the Trinity; they also distort the differences between the Lord in the Old Testament and our Savior in the New. A closer reading of the entire Bible shows remarkable congruency of values across both testaments.

For example, throughout the Old Testament and particularly in the Prophets, we encounter a God who is focused on far more than rituals and sacrifices. Unlike so many pagan deities worshiped by surrounding nations of the time, the God of Israel is not an irritable infant in the sky demanding prayers and offerings to pacify his hot temper. Instead, he seeks worship that goes far beyond songs and ceremonies. In fact, just like Jesus in the Gospels, the God we find in the Old Testament frequently rejects the ritual worship of his people because he desires something more. "These people come near to me with their mouth and honor me with their lips, but their hearts are far from me" (Isa. 29:13).

These words of the Lord through Isaiah are quoted by Jesus centuries later to rebuke the religious people of his day, and for a very similar reason. Jesus doubles down on what God has said he truly desires from his people—our hearts and not merely our words. But what does it mean to have a heart that is far from God?

In modern Christian communities, we use "heart" language when speaking about emotions and passions. Therefore, it's natural to assume that Jesus is scolding people for engaging in stale, perfunctory religious rituals with no genuine feeling. We think a heart far from God is cold, passively engaging in fake, mechanical, unfeeling devotion. This interpretation fits nicely with the common view today that worship should be deeply emotive and spontaneous and that our worship gatherings should kindle fervor in those whose hearts are not sufficiently "on fire" for God. This is why, over the last 150 years, churches have increasingly mimicked the architecture and activities of theaters. They want to make their customers—excuse me, their congregations—*feel something*.

But is that what God means in Isaiah? Is that why Jesus quotes Isaiah to rebuke the religious leaders in first-century Judea? Does God scold us for not having ooey-gooey feelings toward him, as if he's some lovesick, self-absorbed teenager?

A closer reading of Isaiah 29:13 and the Gospel passages where Jesus quotes this verse reveals that he is *not* rebuking the people for their lack of emotional excitement in worship. Instead, he is judging their lack of *justice* toward one another. More specifically, Jesus is appalled that Israel's religious leaders are using their worship of God as an excuse for not fulfilling their obligations to others. They are redirecting resources that should be employed to care for the elderly—*which God commanded them to do!*—and using those resources to create more elaborate worship ceremonies instead (see Matt. 15:3–9).

Likewise, according to Isaiah, the Lord rejects the people's worship because they practice evil, ignore the oppression of immigrants, mistreat the poor, and overlook the needs of orphans and widows. Simply put, they disregard their obligations to those in need, all the while singing praise songs and making offerings to God.

WHAT IF JESUS WAS SERIOUS ABOUT JUSTICE?

So throughout the Bible, we find that a heart far from God doesn't lack emotion or zeal in worship; emotions come and go. God's concern is when our hearts lack empathy and mercy for the suffering. A heart far from God has separated love for God from compassion toward those created in his image. And even worse, a person whose heart is distant from God may even have the audacity to use religious worship as an excuse for not acting justly toward others.

 READ MORE: Isaiah 29:13–21; Matthew 15:3–9

17 IF JESUS WAS SERIOUS ... THEN THE GREATEST COMMANDS ARE ABOUT LOVE, NOT LABELS

RELIGIOUS LEADERS WERE OFTEN testing Jesus. On one occasion, a Bible expert asks him, "Teacher, which is the greatest commandment in the Torah?" Jesus answers by quoting two verses from the Old Testament. "Love the LORD your God with all your heart and with all your soul and with all your strength" (Deut. 6:5), and "Love your neighbor as yourself" (Lev. 19:18). Jesus says that everything else in the Old Testament flows from these two commands (see Matt. 22:34–40).

Notice that Jesus responds to the Bible expert by citing two commandments when he is asked for only one. Why? Because, as we've been exploring, the Bible never separates our vertical relationship with God from our horizontal relationship with people. Our devotion to God is inherently linked to pursuing justice for others. Therefore, when asked for the *single* greatest commandment, Jesus responds with a *double* answer—love the Lord and love your neighbor—because it is impossible to fulfill the former without doing the latter.

Jesus's answer would have been familiar to his original hearers. In fact, linking these two commands was widely done in his culture. In Luke 10, for example, we find another Bible expert citing Deuteronomy 6:5 and Leviticus 19:18 as a summary of the entire Torah, and Jesus praises his answer (Luke 10:28). The Bible expert understands and affirms that his vertical devotion to God is interwoven with his horizontal love for people. But he still has one question for Jesus: *Which* people must he love? "Who is my neighbor?" he asks.

Jesus responds with a story about a man beaten, robbed, and left nearly dead on the side of the road. The first character to pass by is the most respected in Jewish culture—a priest. The second character, a Levite, is also highly admired but slightly below the

HORIZONTAL AND VERTICAL

priest on the social hierarchy. With the introduction of these two characters, Jesus primes his audience to expect the hero of the story to be someone below the Levite. An ordinary Jew without much religious training would have been surprising enough. But when Jesus makes a Samaritan the role model of the story, he doesn't just shock his audience; he deliberately offends them.

Jews despised Samaritans. They were viewed as traitors who had abandoned the true faith of Israel for heretical teachings. This made Samaritans even worse than gentiles, whom the Jews commonly regarded as dogs. The hatred between Jews and Samaritans, which had smoldered for nearly one thousand years, was still white hot in Jesus's day. Certain Jews had destroyed the Samaritan temple, and around AD 6, some Samaritans retaliated by scattering human bones in the Jewish temple during Passover, defiling it so that worship could not be conducted.

It's difficult for us to grasp how outrageous Jesus's story would have been to his audience. Imagine asking a pastor what it means to be a good Christian, and he responds with a story about a merciful Muslim. Or consider the repercussions if a politician was asked what it means to be a true American and they point to an undocumented immigrant. With his story, Jesus is doing more than challenging the Bible expert's definition of "neighbor." He is deconstructing his entire understanding of who truly loves God.

Remember, Jesus's telling of the story of the good Samaritan is in response to a devout Jew asking him what it means to "love your neighbor." The Bible expert has already (and correctly) linked this commandment to the one about loving the Lord. And fully loving God is the key to eternal life in his kingdom. At the time, many saw this as a uniquely Jewish privilege. After all, Jews alone had a covenant with the Lord, possessed his divine laws, and were therefore equipped to obey his commands.

So by making a Samaritan the one in the story who fulfills God's law by caring for the stranger in need, Jesus is subverting his own community's pride and self-image. He is broadening the category of those who truly love God beyond a certain national, ethnic, or even religious identity. And the story reveals that those who possess the right spiritual labels but fail to actually love those in need, like the priest and the Levite, may actually be the ones furthest from God.

 READ MORE: Matthew 22:34–40; Luke 10:25–37

CHRISTIAN KARMA
- WEALTH IS A REWARD FOR RIGHT BEHAVIOR

CHRISTIAN COMPASSION
- WEALTH IS A RESPONSIBILITY TO RIGHT INJUSTICE

18 IF JESUS WAS SERIOUS . . . THEN JUSTICE REQUIRES BOTH COMPASSION AND CAPACITY

THERE ARE NUMEROUS DETAILS in Jesus's story about the good Samaritan that we miss but that would have been significant for his original audience. Among the most emphasized aspects of the story is the wealth of the Samaritan traveler. He is likely a merchant whose business has taken him far from

Samaria. The items he uses to care for the beaten man—wine, oil, and a donkey for transportation—were all expensive goods that only a rich man would possess. When he reaches the inn, the Samaritan pays the innkeeper two denarii to look after the wounded man—enough for more than three weeks of care. And if more money should be needed, he promises to pay the innkeeper upon his return.

The wealth of the Samaritan is important for two reasons. First, while the Samaritan has the *intent* to care for the wounded man (unlike the priest and the Levite), his wealth gives him the *capacity* to actually do it. The story reveals that compassion, while an essential prerequisite for justice, isn't enough by itself. Evil is overcome not just by our warm thoughts but by marshaling resources, coordinating care, and following through over time. These are all seen in the Samaritan's actions. In other words, there is an economic component to justice that many Christian communities overlook.

Second, the Samaritan's wealth is important because he implicitly rejects the prevailing view that wealth is bestowed on the righteous as a reward. The Samaritan could have seen the beaten man on the side of the road and concluded that he deserved his terrible circumstances because of some sin, while he himself enjoyed wealth and comfort because of his righteousness. This view, which was widespread in Jesus's day, remains incredibly common among religious people. I call it "Christian karma." It helps explain why the priest and the Levite pass the beaten man without helping him, and it also helps explain why so many Christians today remain disengaged from caring for the poor and the suffering. Christian karma says everyone is currently receiving exactly what they deserve—both good and bad. Therefore, helping the suffering or sacrificing our comfort is wrong; doing so interferes with God's judgment of the sinful and his rewarding of the righteous.

Jesus repeatedly rejects this logic, and it's completely absent from the Samaritan in his story. The Samaritan does not see his wealth as a reward to be hoarded for self-indulgence. Instead, he sees his wealth as a resource for caring for someone in need. Even more remarkably, the Samaritan knows nothing of the beaten man's identity. Is he a fellow Samaritan? A Jew? A gentile? A Roman? Is he an enemy or an ally? Is the man an innocent victim of criminals, or is he a criminal himself who has gotten what he deserves?

Instead, the only questions the Samaritan asks are: Does this man need my help? and How can I help him?

These observations about Jesus's story are extremely relevant today, as many Christians wonder what seeking justice looks like in our diverse society. As we are made aware of broken systems, inequality, poverty, and pain, many of us feel compassion. But feelings aren't enough. The intent to care must be matched with the capacity to care. Are we, like the Samaritan, willing to sacrifice our resources and sustain our engagement over time to see wrongs made right? And do we see our wealth and resources as divine rewards merely for our own enjoyment or as equipment God has given us to extend his love and justice to others?

 READ MORE: Matthew 19:16–30; Luke 10:25–37

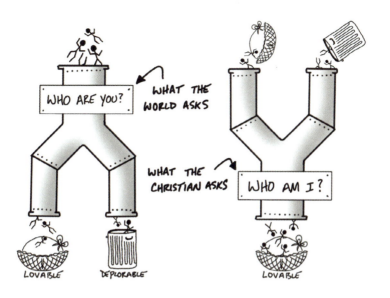

19 IF JESUS WAS SERIOUS . . . THEN JUSTICE IS ABOUT OUR IDENTITY, NOT THE OTHER PERSON'S

A JOURNALIST ONCE ASKED ELIE WIESEL, a Holocaust survivor and writer, "I have noticed that you Jews often answer questions by asking another question. Why do you do that?" Wiesel answered, "Why not?"[1]

The centrality of question asking in the Jewish religious tradition dates back to the ancient world, and it was Jesus's favorite way to teach. In fact, like Wiesel, Jesus often answered a question with more questions. In Luke 10, his engagement with the Bible expert comprises a whole series of questions. The parable itself is told by Jesus in response to the question "Who is my neighbor?" The Bible expert wants to know how precisely to fulfill the commandment to "love your neighbor as yourself" (Lev. 19:18).

Popular teachings at the time said that loving one's neighbor gave implicit permission to hate one's enemy. Another common Jewish teaching instructed, "If you do a kindness, know to whom you do it. . . . Give to the good man, but do not help the sinner" (Sirach 12:1, 7 RSV). Taken together, these interpretations narrowly defined who a "neighbor" was and therefore who was worthy of one's attention and care. Non-Jews and enemies of Israel were clearly not included, but neither were sinful Jews, the irreligious, or anyone who had wronged you. In other words, Jewish tradition had created a circular argument. A neighbor was defined as anyone worthy of my love, and anyone I deemed worthy of my love could rightly be called my neighbor.

This ambiguity is why the Bible expert asks Jesus his question. Precisely who is included in the category of "neighbor," and who is excluded and therefore undeserving of my love? After the story, however, Jesus responds to the man's question with a question of his own. Jesus asks, "Which of these three [the priest, the Levite, or the Samaritan] do you think was a neighbor to the man who fell into the hands of robbers?" (Luke 10:36). Rather than simply offering the man an answer, Jesus, like any good rabbi, wants him to discover the answer for himself.

The Bible expert responds, "The one who had mercy on him" (Luke 10:37). (It's interesting that the Bible expert cannot bring himself to identify the man as "the Samaritan.") Jesus ends the discussion with a simple command: "Go and do likewise" (10:37). This conclusion indicates that the time for questions is over and the time for simple obedience has come.

But notice that, strictly speaking, Jesus does *not* answer the man's original question. He never identifies who the Bible expert's neighbor is. Instead, he asks the man a far more important question: Would *he* be a neighbor to those in need? Jesus's verbal jujitsu is a reminder that sometimes the questions we ask of God aren't the most important ones. While we are preoccupied with others' identity—"Who is my neighbor?"—God is more concerned with our identity. This is because the choice to love another should always be determined by our identity and not that of the person we encounter.

I cannot think of a more relevant lesson for Christians today. In our increasingly diverse, pluralist culture, we are exceedingly preoccupied with boundary questions: Whom should Christian business owners serve? What kind of person should Christians welcome? Which groups should Christians help? With whom

WHAT IF JESUS WAS SERIOUS ABOUT JUSTICE?

should Christians march? Who is worthy of our advocacy? Who deserves religious freedom?

These questions (and many more) all focus on the identity of the other person or group. These questions, like the one asked by the Bible expert, tend to make love, care, and justice contingent on the other person's identity. Are *they* my neighbor? But Jesus invites us to ask a different question: Will *we* be a neighbor to them?

 READ MORE: Matthew 7:15–20; Luke 10:25–37

PART 3

JUDGMENT *AND* MERCY

MATTHEW 12:33–37

Make a tree good and its fruit will be good, or make a tree bad and its fruit will be bad, for a tree is recognized by its fruit. You brood of vipers, how can you who are evil say anything good? For the mouth speaks what the heart is full of. A good man brings good things out of the good stored up in him, and an evil man brings evil things out of the evil stored up in him. But I tell you that everyone will have to give account on the day of judgment for every empty word they have spoken. For by your words you will be acquitted, and by your words you will be condemned.

God is...	Jesus says...
HOLY	BE HOLY AS YOUR HEAVENLY FATHER IS HOLY – MATT. 5:48
MERCIFUL	BE MERCIFUL AS YOUR HEAVENLY FATHER IS MERCIFUL – LUKE 6:36
FORGIVING	FORGIVE AS GOD HAS FORGIVEN YOU – EPH. 4:32
SLOW TO ANGER	HUMAN ANGER DOES NOT PRODUCE RIGHTEOUSNESS – JAMES 1:20
JUDGE OF ALL	DO NOT JUDGE – LUKE 6:37

20 IF JESUS WAS SERIOUS... THEN GOD CAN BE BOTH MERCIFUL AND ANGRY

IN THE OLD TESTAMENT, God describes himself as "slow to anger" (Exod. 34:6). Of course, being slow to anger is very different from never being angry. This fits with popular assumptions about the God of the Old Testament. Even among Christians, it is widely believed that the Lord of the Old Testament is marked by anger and wrath, whereas the Jesus we find in the New Testament emphasizes love and forgiveness. Or put another way, the Old Testament is about judgment, whereas the New Testament is about mercy.

Not only is this an incorrect view of the Bible—God in the Old Testament is described as a nursing mother; Jesus in the New Testament rebukes and overturns tables—but it's also an inaccurate view of God. According to Christian doctrine, the self-description of God we find in the Old Testament must apply equally to all three persons of the Trinity—Father, Son, and Spirit. This means the Lord of the Old Testament is no less gracious and compassionate than the Jesus we find in the New and that Jesus must be as capable of anger and wrath, even if tempered with patience, as the God we read about in the Old. In other words, judgment and mercy are qualities that mark God's character throughout the Bible.

The assumption of a perpetually meek and mild Jesus quickly evaporates upon reading the Gospels. There, we encounter a Jesus who exhibits anger toward his own disciples, overturns tables and brandishes a whip in the temple court, confronts religious leaders with brutal insults, and speaks openly about fearing God and the coming wrath of his judgment. In other words, in Jesus we find the incarnate God of the Old Testament, who is exceedingly gracious and compassionate but who is also capable of righteous anger at abuse and injustice.

Unfortunately, we have trouble holding together these two sides of God's character, and in some Christian communities it has become fashionable to emphasize the anger of Jesus. Tragically, some have come to believe the truly "godly" Christian will be one who is full of wrath toward sin, who condemns every false belief, and who tolerates no unrighteousness. This form of Christianity mistakes anger for passion, excuses judgment as devotion, and sees nonbelievers as enemies to be defeated rather than as neighbors to be loved.

Christians who carry this view of God, in my experience, are vessels of misery. Beneath a facade of piety is a miserable soul determined to infect others with their disease. And when they are confronted for neither behaving like Jesus nor displaying the fruit of his Spirit, their defense is always the same. They cherry-pick a story about Jesus's anger (usually the scene when he flips tables in the temple court) or an apocalyptic symbol from Revelation and then explain the importance of defending the truth in an increasingly anti-Christian age. (Truth is conspicuously absent from the list of the fruit of the Spirit in Galatians 5:22–23. Merely being right or having correct theology isn't evidence of living in unity with God through the indwelling presence of the Holy Spirit.)

Like so many popular errors, this one is constructed on a partial truth. Jesus does display anger, and God's wrath against injustice is vividly seen in the Scriptures. But what pro-anger Christians miss is that nowhere in the New Testament are we commanded to emulate God's wrath, his anger, or his vengeance. These are certainly part of his character, and we can trust that he will wield them redemptively, but we should not trust ourselves. Perhaps that is why Jesus calls us to copy what looms a thousand times larger in our heavenly Father's nature: his mercy. We are to love our enemies as he loves his enemies. We are to forgive as he forgives us. And we are to be merciful as he is merciful.

READ MORE: Exodus 34:5–9; Matthew 21:12–17

21 IF JESUS WAS SERIOUS . . . THEN MERCY AND JUSTICE ARE PARTNERS, NOT ENEMIES

HOW DO WE RECONCILE God's commitment to justice throughout the Bible with his commitment to mercy and forgiveness? First, we must remember that the biblical definition of "justice" is often different from a modern American definition. Popular culture understands justice as the fair enforcement of laws, retributions, and punishments or advocacy for others' fair treatment and acceptance. In other words, justice is often defined *legally*. Biblical justice certainly has a legal component, but in Scripture, justice is fundamentally *relational*. It's about the right ordering of relationships or the restoration of those relationships when they've become disordered so that everyone can flourish.

If we engage the Bible and specifically the teachings of Jesus with our culture's limited, legal understanding of justice, then we will necessarily view mercy and justice as irreconcilable values. For example, I have heard many well-meaning Christian teachers say, "Justice is getting what you deserve. Mercy is *not* getting what you deserve." The problem is that this popular formulation pits two essential aspects of God's character against each other. It assumes that for God to be just, he must reject mercy, and if God shows mercy, then he is not committed to justice.

But in the Bible's ancient cultural context, justice and mercy were not viewed as incompatible. They were not pitted against each other; rather, justice and mercy were understood to be natural allies, not antagonists. Our culture views justice and mercy as antithetical forces, like darkness and light or hot and cold, but in Jesus's culture, justice and mercy were compatible and even cooperative values, more like salt and pepper or peanut butter and jelly.

The ancient biblical culture understood justice as having a relational objective rather than merely a legal one. Therefore, justice could partner with mercy toward the shared goal of restoring human flourishing to a community. So when a violation occurred that brought disorder to a relationship, rather than choosing to

JUDGMENT AND MERCY

respond with either justice or mercy, people followed divine wisdom in their effort to repair and restore the order that was lost, which called for a combination of justice and mercy.

For example, Zacchaeus was a tax collector who defrauded and stole from his neighbors by collecting more taxes than the law required. To restore both his relationship with God and his relationship with his neighbors, Zacchaeus vowed to pay back everyone he'd cheated four times what he had stolen, and Jesus praised him for this commitment (Luke 19:1–10). For Zacchaeus—the one who had violated the law and caused disorder—healing broken relationships required restitution, a central aspect of both biblical and modern justice.

But what if you're the victim? A strictly legal understanding of justice says victims have no responsibility; they are the passive recipients of justice. It is for those in power to enforce the law and for the guilty (like Zacchaeus) to make restitution. But if we see justice biblically—as the restoration of properly ordered relationships—then Jesus's many commands about forgiveness begin to make sense. Jesus invites victims to take an active role in restoring order and flourishing by practicing mercy. Mercy, therefore, is not opposed to justice but is its indispensable partner in healing our broken world.

 READ MORE: Luke 19:1–10; Colossians 3:12–14

22 IF JESUS WAS SERIOUS... THEN OUR MERCY, LIKE GOD'S, SHOULD EXCEED ALL EXPECTATIONS

MANY PEOPLE APPROACH RELIGION the way they approach their taxes. All they want to know is the minimum amount required of them, what loopholes apply, and how to avoid closer scrutiny. The goal is to do, give, or pray just enough to meet God's expectations—but not an ounce more.

Many who question Jesus in the Gospels have this minimum-standard mindset. Peter reveals this attitude when he asks Jesus, "Lord, how many times shall I forgive my brother or sister who sins against me? Up to seven times?" (Matt. 18:21). To be fair to Peter, a popular rabbinical teaching in his day was that forgiveness was required three times. Peter must have known that Jesus often called for mercy that far exceeded what was common in their religious and social contexts, so Peter more than doubles the forgiveness quota to seven times. Still, whether three or seven, Peter is looking for the lowest number necessary to pass God's expectation of forgiveness.

Jesus's response must have shocked Peter. "No, not seven times . . . but seventy times seven!" (Matt. 18:22 NLT). Reading Jesus literally would mean forgiving someone 490 times, but that would be missing his point. Jesus's hyperbolic math is meant to communicate that among his followers, forgiveness is to be limitless.

Peter and the other apostles would have recognized two Old Testament echoes in Jesus's answer. First, when God proclaimed his name and described his character to Moses on Mount Sinai, he included two sets of numbers. The Lord said he would punish sin "to the third and fourth," but he would forgive and maintain love "to thousands" (Exod. 34:7).[1] The point is simple and powerful. The numbers three and four are much, much smaller than a thousand. The Lord is declaring that he is just and will punish evil, but his wrath reaches only three or four on the scale, whereas his mercy, forgiveness, and love are off the charts. Jesus is saying something similar in his response to Peter. Just as God's forgiveness far outweighs his wrath, so should ours.

The second and more explicit echo comes from Genesis 4, where the Lord vows to seek vengeance "seven times" on anyone who kills Cain (v. 15). Generations later, Cain's descendant Lamech says, "If Cain is avenged seven times, then Lamech seventy-seven times" (v. 24). The story illustrates the violent escalation of vengeance that marked so much of the ancient world and that still infects too many societies. By referencing these words from Genesis, Jesus inverts the vow of Lamech. Whereas excessive vengeance is often embraced without limits, Jesus is declaring that among his followers, forgiveness must be practiced without limits.

Beyond being a jaw-dropping call to unlimited forgiveness, Jesus's answer is also a rebuke of Peter's search for God's minimum requirements. Those who are looking to win God's favor by exhibiting the least amount of mercy necessary have clearly not yet been transformed by his grace.

 READ MORE: Matthew 18:21–22; Ephesians 4:29–32

23 IF JESUS WAS SERIOUS . . . THEN JUSTICE ALONE WON'T RESCUE US FROM OUR SINS

IN RESPONSE TO PETER'S QUESTION about forgiveness, Jesus tells another parable. The story is about a king settling his accounts with his servants. The scenario would have been familiar to Jesus's first-century audience. Kings collected taxes from their subjects by hiring financial ministers or governors to collect money on their behalf. In turn, these ministers and governors hired tax collectors in towns and villages. These roles were very lucrative because only a portion of the funds collected were paid up the chain of command, with those at each level pocketing some of the revenue for themselves.

One of the king's servants in Jesus's story owes an astronomical amount of money—ten thousand talents. For some perspective, a talent equaled ten thousand denarii. One denarius was the normal pay for a single day's work. Therefore, the man's debt was *one hundred million denarii*. A first-century historian reports that the entire tax debt of Galilee, Judea, and Samaria was six hundred talents, but in Jesus's story, one man owes ten thousand![1] Clearly, Jesus is using an inconceivable number to make a point.

Because the man is unable to pay the debt, the king orders the man, his wife, and his children to be sold into slavery and all his property liquidated. The servant, however, falls on his knees before the king and begs for more time to repay his debt. Of course, this is ridiculous. No amount of time will ever be enough to repay ten thousand talents. Likewise, religious traditions that claim the debt of sin can be repaid with prayers, good works, and meritorious rituals are also delusional. Jesus's parable is intended to show the inescapable magnitude of our sins, the utter hopelessness of our position. We can do nothing to free ourselves from sin's grasp.

The story illustrates the limits of justice. Justice alone would insist that the man repay what he owes, but Jesus's story shows that

JUDGMENT AND MERCY

true restoration is sometimes impossible without mercy playing a role. Until we grasp the depth of our sin, we will never recognize the true scale of God's mercy. In the story, the king is filled with compassion for the servant, and rather than merely granting him more time to repay, as justice would dictate—a useless gesture anyway—the king cancels the debt entirely. In the cosmic economy of God's kingdom, we are powerless to repay our debts, but thanks be to God, for he is merciful to all who humbly fall before him.

 READ MORE: Matthew 18:23–35; 6:14–15

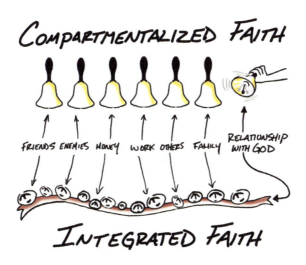

24 IF JESUS WAS SERIOUS... THEN GOD'S MERCY COMES WITH A CONDITION

TO EXPLAIN THE NATURE OF GOD'S MERCY, Jesus tells a story about a servant who owes his king one hundred million denarii. After the man begs for more time to pay, the king extends mercy to the man by completely forgiving his astronomical debt. The twist in the parable comes when the forgiven man encounters a fellow servant who owes him just one hundred denarii. The proportions are important to notice. The amount owed to the servant is an infinitesimal amount compared to his own debt forgiven by the king. However, when the man owing just one hundred denarii begs for mercy, the servant offers none. Instead, he demands repayment in full.

When word reaches the king, he is furious. "You wicked servant," he blasted. "I canceled all that debt of yours because you begged me to. Shouldn't you have had mercy on your fellow servant just as I had on you?" (Matt. 18:32–33). The king rescinds his mercy, reinstates the man's one-hundred-million-denarii debt, and throws him in jail. Jesus concludes with a sober warning: "This is how my heavenly Father will treat each of you unless you forgive your brother or sister from your heart" (18:35).

The parable is a challenge to our private, individualized view of faith. We have been shaped by a religious culture that emphasizes having a "personal relationship with God." By this we often mean a relationship with God that is hermetically sealed off from any other person or community. As a result, we assume faith is something we engage privately and that receiving God's forgiveness and mercy is unrelated to anything or anyone else.

Here's one way to understand this compartmentalization. In the modern world, we often view different parts of our lives like a set of handbells. Family, work, sports, faith, and numerous other activities and relationships are each a different bell. We pick up and ring the God bell when we pray, read our Bible, or attend a worship gathering, but this does not impact any other bell. Therefore, seeking God's mercy and forgiveness for my sins does not require me to examine or reevaluate any other relationship. But Jesus rejects this separation. With his parable, he is saying that our lives are more like a string of sleigh bells. Ringing one will effectively ring them all. Our relationship with God must reverberate through every part of our lives and every relationship.

Jesus's story obliterates hyperindividualism and the common view that God's mercy carries no conditions. We've already explored how our vertical relationship with God is intertwined with our horizontal relationships with others, and with this parable, Jesus makes clear that mercy is not exempt from this dynamic. In fact, receiving God's mercy comes with the expectation that we will extend mercy to others and that failing to do so will necessarily result in damaging our right relationship with God.

 READ MORE: Matthew 18:21–35; Colossians 3:13

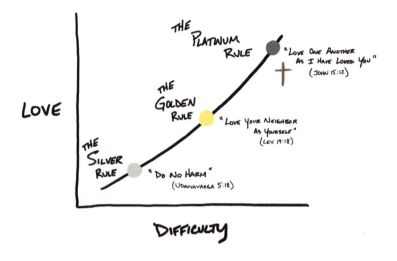

25 IF JESUS WAS SERIOUS...
THEN WE WILL BE JUDGED BY A HIGHER STANDARD THAN THE GOLDEN RULE

MANY PEOPLE IN A PLURALISTIC SOCIETY assert that all religious traditions are more or less the same and often point to the Golden Rule as a universal value found in all religions. That is partly correct. The Golden Rule, as taught by Jesus, is a call to actively seek the welfare of others: "So in everything, do to others what you would have them do to you" (Matt. 7:12).

Hinduism, Buddhism, and Confucianism have parallel teachings, but they are passive by comparison. Rather than saying we should actively seek to bless others, the sacred texts of these religions say we should merely "do no harm" to others. For example, Udanavarga 5:18, cited by both Hindus and Buddhists, says, "Hurt not others in ways that you yourself would find hurtful."[1] If the Golden Rule means actively loving others as ourselves, then we might call this less-elevated command not to hurt others the Silver Rule.

Of course, as commendable as the Golden Rule is, Jesus does not stop there. On a number of occasions, he calls his disciples to an even *higher* command—what some have called the Platinum Rule. For example, Jesus tells his followers, "As I have loved you, so you must love one another" (John 13:34). Here the standard is not human kindness but divine love. Likewise, Jesus commands us to love our enemies because God also loves his enemies (Matt. 5:43–48). If left with the Golden Rule alone, we might conclude that ignoring or avoiding our enemies is sufficient. After all, that may be what we want our enemies to do to us. But the Platinum Rule requires us to actively love our adversaries, not merely bypass them.

So we have this three-tiered understanding of how we are called to treat others:

Silver = Do No Harm
Gold = Love like Self
Platinum = Love like God

With these commandments in mind, we can begin to see what is so shocking about Jesus's parable of the unforgiving servant. Strictly speaking, when the servant whose debt of one hundred million denarii is forgiven refuses to forgive the minor one-hundred-denarii debt of his fellow servant, he is following the Silver Rule. He is not actively harming the man but simply allowing him to face the natural consequences of his failure to pay. In a similar way, in the story of the good Samaritan, the priest and the Levite may not help the man beaten by robbers, but they don't seek his harm either. They, too, are adhering to the Silver Rule.

Applying the Golden Rule—love your neighbor as yourself—increases expectations. In this case, the forgiven servant should have shown his fellow servant leniency by giving him more time to repay his one-hundred-denarii debt. After all, this is precisely what he desired for himself. He had asked the king for more time to repay the one hundred million denarii he owed. Failing to adhere to the Golden Rule, however, is not the standard by which the king ultimately judges the unmerciful servant.

The powerful message of Jesus's parable is that the servant fails to follow the Platinum Rule; he does not forgive his fellow servant's debt in the same way the king has forgiven his. The great sin of the unmerciful servant isn't that he doesn't love others as himself but that he doesn't love others *as the king has loved him*.

Loving others just as God has loved us is what separates the call of Christ from that of others and what elevates his gospel to a higher moral code than other religious messages. He calls us to much more than not inflicting harm, even more than loving our neighbors as ourselves. We are to love others with the same love that our heavenly Father has lavished on us—a love that is infinite in depth and unyielding in mercy.

 READ MORE: Matthew 18:23–35; Luke 6:27–36

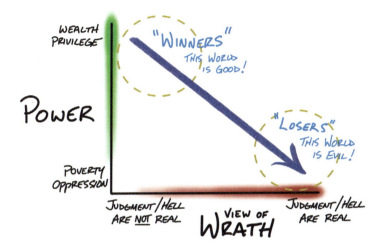

26 IF JESUS WAS SERIOUS . . . THEN GOD IS WRATHFUL BECAUSE HE IS LOVING

FEW THINGS MAKE BOTH BELIEVERS and nonbelievers more uncomfortable than the idea of the wrath of God. It conjures images of fire-and-brimstone preachers, Dante's *Inferno*, and a judgmental form of religion that many people in a therapeutic culture find intolerable. As a result, we mostly avoid speaking about God's wrath in favor of his polite attributes. But this isn't true of everyone.

To be clear, minimizing divine anger and worshiping a god without wrath are so often impulses of the comfortable and powerful. Those who have not experienced war, hunger, abuse, or oppression can easily erase God's wrath and feel no loss, but that is not true for those who have intensely experienced the injustice of the world. Could this help explain recent data that white Christians in the United States are much less likely than black Christians to believe in hell and God's judgment of sin?[1] Could belonging to a historically powerful group lead us to downplay the importance of God's wrath against injustice, and could belonging to a historically marginalized group lead us to value this doctrine?

Miroslav Volf used to minimize God's wrath in favor of a one-dimensional God of love. That was until the Bosnian War destroyed his homeland. He writes:

> I used to think that wrath was unworthy of God. Isn't God love? Shouldn't divine love be beyond wrath? God is love, and God loves every person and every creature. That's exactly why God is wrathful against some of them. My last resistance to the idea of God's wrath was a casualty of the war in former Yugoslavia, the region from which I come. According to some estimates, 200,000 people were killed and over 3,000,000 were displaced. My villages and cities were destroyed, my people shelled day

in and day out, some of them brutalized beyond imagination, and I could not imagine God not being angry.

Or think of Rwanda in the last decade of the past century, where 800,000 people were hacked to death in one hundred days! How did God react to the carnage? By doting on the perpetrators in a grandparently fashion? By refusing to condemn the bloodbath but instead affirming the perpetrators' basic goodness? Wasn't God fiercely angry with them? Though I used to complain about the indecency of the idea of God's wrath, I came to think that I would have to rebel against a God who *wasn't* wrathful at the sight of the world's evil. God isn't wrathful in spite of being love. God is wrathful *because* God is love.[2]

Volf's account is a reminder that we need to listen to our sisters and brothers around the world and across history about the significance of God's wrath. If we live in relative tranquility, we ought to be grateful for our circumstances, but we must not allow our distance from injustice to warp our perception of God and his character. We must hear from those who know the world's pain because they illuminate for us a facet of our faith and God's nature that we might otherwise miss. If we don't want to erase God's wrath or minimize his justice, then we must not silence the voices of those crying out for it.

 READ MORE: Ezekiel 33:10–11; Nahum 1:2–6

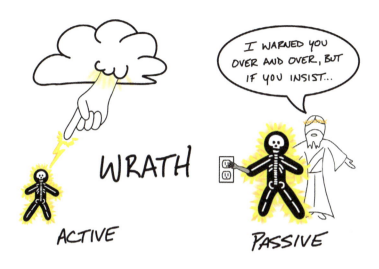

27 IF JESUS WAS SERIOUS . . . THEN GOD'S WRATH IS USUALLY PASSIVE, NOT ACTIVE

MODERN AMERICAN CHURCHES often ignore large sections of Scripture, and many people have their beliefs shaped more by popular Christian music than by the Bible or church doctrine. To be fair, many worship songs are wonderful, inspiring, and theologically faithful. The problem is that the music we sing in many church gatherings covers a narrow slice of biblical ideas. Countless songs exist about God's love, goodness, and mercy, but have you ever heard a worship chorus about his judgment?

The Bible contains more than six hundred verses about divine wrath. It's not a minor or peripheral theme in the Bible because, as we've seen, God's justice saturates both the Old and the New Testaments. In fact, justice is central to his mission to free his people and all of creation from evil by putting everything back into its proper order. I like how John Stott defines God's wrath. He says it is God's "unrelenting, unremitting, uncompromising, and steadfast antagonism towards evil in all its forms."[1] Isn't that precisely the kind of God we want and need?

But it's important to recognize that God's wrath against evil does not always take the same form. Theologians differentiate between God's active and passive wrath. Active wrath is when God directly intervenes to stop an unjust act or to condemn those doing it. We see this in Acts 5 when Ananias and Sapphira immediately fall dead after deceiving the apostles about their charity. Such stories get a lot of attention, and they're usually the ones cited by critics of the Christian faith who want to dismiss God as a moral monster, but such stories are exceedingly rare in the Bible. Far more often, we see God's wrath expressed passively.

Passive wrath is when God allows us to experience the natural consequences of our rebellious, evil actions. Many of Jesus's statements are rooted in this understanding of God's judgment. For example, he often compares people to trees, saying, "No good tree bears bad fruit, nor does a bad tree bear good fruit. Each tree is recognized by its own fruit" (Luke 6:43–44). And he tells multiple parables about unfruitful trees or branches being thrown out and burned.

Likewise, when Jesus foretells the destruction of Jerusalem (which occurred in AD 70), he says, "Jerusalem, Jerusalem, you who kill the prophets and stone those sent to you, how often I have longed to gather your children together, as a hen gathers her chicks under her wings, and you were not willing. Look, your house is left to you desolate" (Matt. 23:37–38). In this case, Jesus says Jerusalem has both rejected God's mercy and faced the natural consequences for its generations of injustice. In all these examples, Jesus echoes a common theme found throughout the Bible: everyone reaps what they sow (see Gal. 6:7).

God mercifully protects us from the horrors of our sins; he is always holding down the lid on the boiling cauldron of evil we have brewed. Eventually, however, when we have refused his warnings and rejected his love long enough, he says to us, in effect, "Very well, *your* will be done." He then steps aside and removes his merciful hand from the lid, allowing the full destructive power of our own evil to overflow upon us.

Often, this passive form of wrath is described in Scripture as the Lord "giving people over" to the natural consequences of their desires. For example, the apostle Paul says in Romans, "The wrath of God is being revealed from heaven against all the godlessness and wickedness of people" (1:18). How is God's wrath revealed? In the verses that follow, Paul says three times that "God gave them over" to their "sinful desires," to "shameful lusts," and to "a depraved mind" (vv. 24, 26, 28). Paul says that God's wrath is revealed when he does not interfere or protect us from our own evil choices (see also Ezek. 20).

Many people are uncomfortable with the idea of divine wrath because they think it means God is unforgiving and unmerciful, but the intent of God's wrath is precisely the opposite. Once we come to see that his wrath is giving sinful people what they want, we will discover that it isn't the Lord who is harsh and unmerciful; rather, it is sin. When we experience the natural consequences of our own wickedness, we discover what a brutal and unforgiving master it is. By shielding us from these natural consequences, God is revealing his compassion and mercy. But sometimes these same attributes cause him to take the shield away in the hope that once we experience the bitter fruit of our evil, we will turn from our wickedness and discover the goodness of life with him.

Abraham Lincoln understood the American Civil War as an instance of God's passive wrath. In his second inaugural address, he said the war was God's judgment on the country for the evil of slavery, but this judgment did not come in the form of direct, active wrath. God did not send fire from heaven to consume the United States like Sodom and Gomorrah. Nor did he spontaneously strike six hundred thousand Americans dead like Ananias and Sapphira.

JUDGMENT AND MERCY

Instead, he allowed the United States to experience the bitter fruit of its devotion to injustice and slavery. The war would continue, Lincoln said, "until all the wealth piled by the bondservant's two hundred and fifty years of unrequited toil shall be sunk and until every drop of blood drawn with the lash shall be paid by another drawn with the sword; as was said three thousand years ago, so still it must be said, 'The judgments of the Lord are true and righteous altogether.'"[2]

Ultimately, God's wrath reveals our cruelty, not God's. And it doesn't diminish God's mercy. Can we be angry at God for his wrath when, in almost every case, he's merely allowing us to experience the effects of what we have chosen? Is it fair to accuse our heavenly Father of cruelty after he has extended to us countless chances to repent and after he's protected us from ourselves for so long? The real problem isn't that we're uncomfortable with God's wrath; it's that we're too comfortable with our propensity for evil.

 READ MORE: Acts 5:1–11; Romans 1:18–32

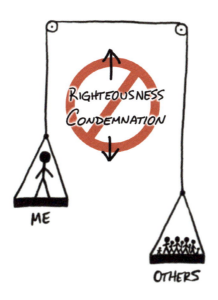

28 IF JESUS WAS SERIOUS . . . THEN GOD'S MERCY WILL MAKE THE SELF-RIGHTEOUS ANGRY

JESUS'S STORY ABOUT A MAN with two sons explores the tension we feel between mercy and judgment. The younger son disrespects his father, demands his inheritance early, leaves home, and squanders his wealth on wild self-indulgence. When the young man eventually finds himself broke, homeless, and hungry, he decides to return home. Remarkably, rather than scolding his foolish son, the father shows him extravagant mercy. He runs out, embraces his son, and throws a party to celebrate his return.

The older son, who has been hard at work this whole time, calls one of the servants and asks about the music and dancing. "Your brother has come home," the servant says, "and your father has killed the fattened calf because he has him back safe and sound" (Luke 15:27). When the older son hears this, he becomes angry and refuses to go in. His anger, as he explains later in the story, is rooted in his desire for justice. His younger brother is a sinner who deserves punishment, not a party. The older son, who has always obeyed his father, is the one who should be rewarded.

By stewing in his anger and refusing to join the party, the older son in Jesus's parable recalls the prophet Jonah. In the Old Testament, Jonah refuses to go to Nineveh as the Lord has commanded him, and when God is later merciful toward that sinful city, it displeases Jonah, and he is angry. "That is what I tried to forestall by fleeing to Tarshish," Jonah complains. "I knew that you are a gracious and compassionate God, slow to anger and abounding in love" (Jon. 4:2). Jonah then asks the Lord to kill him, "for it is better for me to die than to live," he says (4:3). The prophet would rather die than live in a world where sinners are forgiven by God.

Both the older son in the parable and the prophet Jonah display a common quality among the self-righteous: God's mercy makes them mad. It's one of the surest ways to spot those who fundamentally misunderstand divine justice. The self-righteous forget that God's justice is always restorative before it is ever punitive, because his primary desire is to restore his relationship with his children. This is why the father in the parable runs out and embraces his wayward son.

Many religious people today fixate on the punitive dimension of justice. They carefully keep score of everyone's good and bad behavior, then heap scorn, shame, and condemnation on the worst transgressors. It sounds like a miserable way to live, but it carries a hidden benefit. By clearly defining who is wrong and sinful, we get to feel righteous and holy about ourselves. Such a feeling helps explain why the older son and Jonah react so negatively when God responds to the guilty with compassion. Mercy violates and deconstructs their own sense of righteous superiority. They wrongly believe that their elevation requires another's condemnation. The older son refuses to join the party because doing so will require surrendering his sense of superiority, and Jonah would rather die than see himself as needing the same mercy as the sinful people of Nineveh.

But is it wrong to want justice? Is it ungodly to want evil punished and good rewarded? Of course not. As we've already seen, the Bible says a lot about God's wrath toward evil. And throughout the Scriptures, the oppressed cry out to God for justice against their enemies. The real question to ask ourselves is this: *Why* do I want justice?

WHAT IF JESUS WAS SERIOUS ABOUT JUSTICE?

Is it because I ache over the evil in the world and for those hurt by it? Or do I want justice because when the guilty are condemned, my own sense of righteousness rises? Do I want justice because I desire the healing and restoration of broken relationships and communities or because I feel those who've done wrong are unworthy of the status I desire for myself? If you're unsure about your motives, consider this question: If God were to forgive the person you despise the most, would you join the celebration? See, there's some Jonah in all of us.

 READ MORE: Jonah 4:1–11; Luke 15:11–32

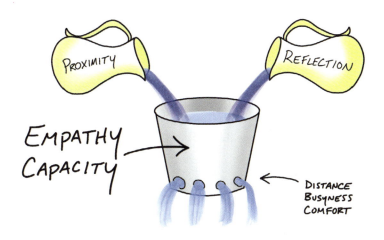

29. IF JESUS WAS SERIOUS... THEN EMPATHY HEALS ARROGANCE AND JUDGMENTALISM

IN JESUS'S STORY ABOUT THE MAN with two sons, the older son refuses to join the party after the return of his younger brother. His reason is simple: his obedient behavior should be celebrated, and his brother's sinful behavior should not. In his view, the two young men belong to different categories and share nothing in common. With this wall of separation firmly in place, the older son has cut off his own ability to empathize with his brother. He's not alone.

A 2012 study authored by a team of psychologists has shown that empathy had declined dramatically in the United States over the previous thirty years.[1] To understand why, we first need to recognize the basic ingredients necessary for empathy. Mark Honigsbaum notes, "Decades of scientific research show that people are kinder . . . when we make the imaginative effort to step into the shoes of another person and see things from their perspective. [Then] we become less capable of ignoring their suffering."[2]

Other studies have found that when people are rushed, their capacity to show empathy severely decreases. Such a finding makes perfect sense. We are less likely to expend imaginative effort if our minds are frantically occupied with other tasks or if we are constantly distracted.[3] One study also found that as people achieve more wealth and status, they feel significantly less empathy toward those with less wealth or status.[4] This may be simple coldheartedness, but it's more likely a result of *distance*. In America, gaining wealth means isolating oneself from those in poverty and hardship. It's much more difficult to put yourself in the shoes of a person you never see because you live in a gated community.

This data helps explain America's growing empathy deficit. Over the past several decades, Americans have grown increasingly busy, stressed, and distracted, and we've become more stratified as a society, with a shrinking middle class leaving a widening gap between the wealthy and the poor. Sociologists also blame what they call "the Big Sort," the trend among Americans to relocate to communities of like-minded people.[5] This trend means that we are less likely to personally know or live near people who vote, worship, or live differently than we do.

Taking all of this together, it appears we are rapidly losing the two ingredients necessary for an empathic culture: mental space and physical proximity. Even worse, the space that empathy once occupied is quickly filled with snap judgments and casual condemnation. It's far easier to denounce "those people" when we do not consider any of them "our people." Judgments are rarer and sometimes hindered altogether when we know a person's entire story, their context, and the nuances of their circumstances—the very things we lose with distance and distraction.

These ingredients for empathy add some nuance to Jesus's story. The older brother is very busy in the fields overseeing the family business (distracted), and his younger brother has been gone a long time in a foreign country (distance). The older son's capacity for empathy has diminished, while his self-righteousness and judgmentalism have grown. Of course, one can also move in the other direction. Our capacity to empathize can grow if we draw closer to others and dare to imagine ourselves in their shoes.

This reality is precisely what makes the Christian message, when properly understood, so necessary in our divided society.

No division is greater than the one between God and humanity, between creature and Creator, between the Holy One and the sinful. And yet the gospel is all about God overcoming this distance to be with us. John says that, in Jesus, God came to make his home among us (John 1:14).

But the Christian story deals with more than just God's physical proximity. God also came to share in our sufferings, to step into our shoes. Paul says that Jesus willingly emptied himself and made himself nothing (Phil. 2:7). The writer of Hebrews emphasizes Jesus's empathy for us as our "brother"—a fellow human. Jesus understands our weaknesses and temptations. He has shared in our sufferings (Heb. 2:10–18). Therefore, he does not stand apart from us, casting judgment and condemning our failures, like the older brother in the parable. Instead, full of empathy and understanding, he joyfully joins the party to welcome us home.

 READ MORE: Luke 15:11–32; Hebrews 2:10–18

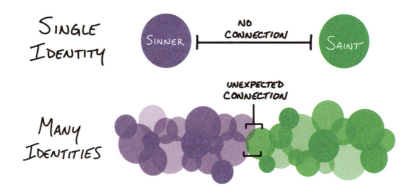

30 IF JESUS WAS SERIOUS . . . THEN WE CAN'T REDUCE PEOPLE TO A SINGLE STORY OR SIN

WE LIVE IN A PUNITIVE SOCIETY where our sins are not easily forgiven or forgotten and where vengeance is often confused with justice. Instant digital communication allows an impulsive comment or indiscreet photo to spread rapidly and linger painfully. (I'm grateful social media did not exist when I was a teenager.) And our criminal justice system has made it very difficult for those with past offenses to find a fresh start. Many carry a permanent scarlet letter blocking them from employment, housing, education, or voting.

Peter was guilty of a terrible sin. On the night Jesus was arrested, Peter repeatedly denied even knowing his Lord in order to protect himself and his reputation, and he did this after vowing that he would never abandon Jesus. For his disloyalty, Peter deserved to be condemned by Jesus, shunned by the other disciples, stripped of his leadership role, and banished from the community. He could have carried the shame of his sin for the rest of his days, but he did not. After the resurrection, Jesus forgave Peter for his denials and restored his status among the apostles.

The world wants to label us according to our sins and failures, but as Bryan Stevenson, author of *Just Mercy* and founder of the Equal Justice Initiative, says, "Each of us is more than the worst thing we've ever done."[1] Jesus always sees more than our mistakes. He sees a person created in the image of God who can be redeemed from their past. This is why he befriended cheats, sinners, adulterers, and thieves, and it is why he was able to look at the men murdering him and pray, "Father, forgive them" (Luke 23:34).

Just as we are each more than the worst thing we've ever done, we are also more than a single label. We tend to see those we disagree with through a simplistic, tainted lens. The philosopher Amartya Sen calls this tendency "miniaturization."[2] Rather than seeing our dissenters as complicated, multidimensional people, we reduce them to a one-dimensional identity that is often based

JUDGMENT AND MERCY

on a negative or an exaggerated quality. They are merely liberal or conservative, woke or alt-right, a snowflake or a fascist.

Miniaturization causes us to ignore the many points at which our identity overlaps with that of our dissenters, to instead focus on the single point where we diverge. It's an effective strategy employed by political and media figures to cultivate fear of enemies rather than love of neighbors.

Miniaturization is also a serious obstacle to justice. When we see only what makes another person dissimilar to us, a desire for justice can deteriorate into a desire for mere vengeance. Remember, biblical justice is about the restoration of properly ordered relationships. Vengeance, in contrast, is about punishment and repayment for evil. Failing to recognize any part of ourselves in the other person, as we've already seen, prevents the cultivation of empathy, and that quickly untethers justice from compassion. All we then recognize is that we are right and they are wrong; we are righteous and they are wicked. We see only their sin and never their larger self. From that point, we will find it impossible to pursue the kind of restorative justice Jesus showed Peter or the forgiveness he offered his executioners.

If we are to emulate God's justice, we must resist the temptation to reduce people—including our enemies—to a single story, a single identity, or a single sin.

 READ MORE: Matthew 26:69–75; John 21:15–19

PART 4

VICTORY *AND* DEFEAT

JOHN 12:23-33

Jesus replied, "The hour has come for the Son of Man to be glorified. Very truly I tell you, unless a kernel of wheat falls to the ground and dies, it remains only a single seed. But if it dies, it produces many seeds. Anyone who loves their life will lose it, while anyone who hates their life in this world will keep it for eternal life. Whoever serves me must follow me; and where I am, my servant also will be. My Father will honor the one who serves me.

"Now my soul is troubled, and what shall I say? 'Father, save me from this hour'? No, it was for this very reason I came to this hour. Father, glorify your name!"

Then a voice came from heaven, "I have glorified it, and will glorify it again." The crowd that was there and heard it said it had thundered; others said an angel had spoken to him.

Jesus said, "This voice was for your benefit, not mine. Now is the time for judgment on this world; now the prince of this world will be driven out. And I, when I am lifted up from the earth, will draw all people to myself." He said this to show the kind of death he was going to die.

31. IF JESUS WAS SERIOUS... THEN THE CROSS HAS COSMIC IMPLICATIONS

WHAT STORY ARE THE GOSPELS trying to tell us?

A few years ago, a pastor told me the convicting story of a South Asian man from a Hindu background who had started attending his church with some regularity. After a few months, the man set up a meeting with the pastor. "The church has been so welcoming," he reported to the pastor. "The music has been excellent, and my children love their classes. I have learned a lot about relationships and leadership and how to manage my money. But tell me, when am I going to learn about Jesus?"

In many enclaves of American Christianity, we behave as if the Gospel stories are divinely inspired self-improvement guides. We assume our struggles in life are the result of employing a flawed strategy rather than the result of our captivity to and cooperation with evil. Through this therapeutic lens, Jesus's death and resurrection are seen as final proof of his authority and evidence that we ought to take his teachings seriously. And we certainly should! But for too many, the meaning of the cross ends there. Any larger, cosmic significance to the cross is lost because in much of consumeristic Christianity, the customer is king. We see ourselves and our problems as the center of the universe. Therefore, we assume what Jesus did on the cross was merely for our individual benefit.

If we are to properly understand Jesus's cross, we must not diminish the reality of evil, the captivity of all creation to sin, and the unstoppable tenacity of God's justice. And we certainly must not reduce the gospel to a consumeristic vision of self-improvement. New Testament scholar N. T. Wright says, "The story the Gospels are trying to tell us is a story in which evil and its deadly power are taken utterly seriously, over against the tendency in many quarters today to cling on to an older liberal idea that there wasn't really much wrong with the world or with human beings in the first place." On the cross, "Jesus suffers the full consequences of evil:

VICTORY AND DEFEAT

evil from the political, social, cultural, personal, moral, religious and spiritual angles all rolled into one."[1]

If we fail to see evil and God's judgment of it as serious realities, then we will fail to see the cross as the good news that the Gospels present it to be. In other words, every time we diminish the reality of evil and the tenacity of God's justice, we inadvertently diminish the cross of Christ as well.

 READ MORE: 1 Corinthians 15:20–28; Colossians 1:15–23

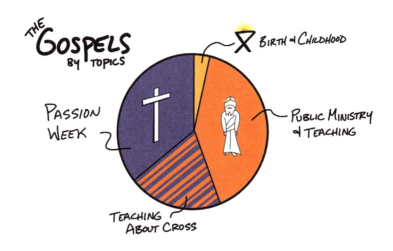

32 IF JESUS WAS SERIOUS . . . THEN JESUS'S CROSS IS BAD NEWS BEFORE IT IS GOOD NEWS

WE'VE SEEN HOW JUSTICE IS CENTRAL to God's character and mission. It forms the foundation of the Old Testament stories and commands, and the Gospel writers draw from these stories and commands to explain Jesus's messianic identity and work. But what about the cross? How does a biblical understanding of God's justice help us make sense of Jesus's self-sacrificial death?

WHAT IF JESUS WAS SERIOUS ABOUT JUSTICE?

This is not an insignificant question. After all, each Gospel devotes more space to the events surrounding Jesus's death on the cross than to anything else. Nearly half of Matthew, Mark, and Luke focus on the final days of Jesus's life, and two-thirds of the Gospel of John is about the last week of Jesus's life.[1] Therefore, if we are going to have a truly Christian understanding of justice, we must wrestle with what the cross of Christ tells us about it.

It's essential first to underscore that the Bible does not neatly divide people or groups into categories of innocent and guilty, or oppressed and oppressors. Remember, the Israelites were enslaved and victimized by the Egyptians in the Old Testament, but God's law also instructed them not to mistreat foreigners themselves—which is precisely what they later did. Scripture does not present God's people merely as victims of evil; we are also perpetrators of it.

G. K. Chesterton captures this truth succinctly in response to a writing contest sponsored by the *London Times*, which asked, "What's wrong with the world?" Chesterton reportedly sent the shortest essay:

Dear Sirs:
I am.

Sincerely yours,
G. K. Chesterton[2]

VICTORY AND DEFEAT

Since the earliest years of the church, theologians have correctly understood the cross as the place where Jesus redeemed the world by defeating the powers aligned against God and his ordering of creation. Many of our songs and hymns celebrate the cross for this reason. It represents the great victory of Jesus. But if *I* am what's wrong with the world and a perpetrator of injustice, not just an innocent victim of it, then the cross must hold another dimension that we don't usually sing about. The cross is not only where Jesus *saved* me from evil but also where he *defeated* me as an agent of evil. It is where he once and for all cast me down as a would-be usurper of God's throne.

This is not how most have been taught to think about Jesus's cross. We prefer to fixate on the cross as the vehicle of our salvation, not as the instrument of our destruction. But God's restorative justice requires both. As the apostle Paul makes clear in his Letter to the Romans, the cross cannot save us from evil if it does not simultaneously condemn our evil (see Rom. 6:1–10).

Frederick Buechner says, "The Gospel is bad news before it is good news."[3] Before we can claim to be saved and brought to new life by Jesus's death, we must first be willing to accept that we are condemned by it, that our old self—with its addiction to evil; its bent toward disorder, chaos, and injustice; and its sinful desire to occupy God's rightful place over creation—has been judged, convicted, and killed.

 READ MORE: Romans 6:1–6; Colossians 2:8–15

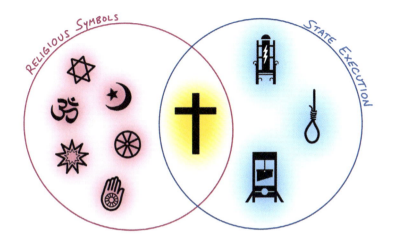

33 IF JESUS WAS SERIOUS... THEN THE UGLINESS OF THE CROSS REVEALS GOD'S GOODNESS

AMONG WORLD RELIGIONS, Christianity has a highly unusual symbol. Islam's crescent moon is meant to symbolize the holy month of Ramadan. Buddhism's wheel represents transformation and reincarnation. The lotus flower is used in Baha'i to symbolize clarity and harmony. Although the exact origin of the Star of David, associated with Judaism, is unknown, it is also, at least at face value, inoffensive, even if it has been employed by anti-Semites in deeply offensive ways. Moons, stars, flowers, and wheels are simple and serene. The Christian cross is not. It's a symbol of humiliation, judgment, and death. In fact, crosses were considered repulsive in the ancient world. As theologian Fleming Rutledge notes,

> The Roman world was largely unanimous that crucifixion was a horrific, disgusting business. . . . The relative scarcity of references to crucifixions in antiquity . . . are less a historical problem than an aesthetic one. . . . Crucifixion was widespread and frequent, above all in Roman times, but the cultured literary world wanted to have nothing to do with it, and as a rule kept quiet about it.[1]

This discomfort with the cross persists among some Christians today. Although Jesus's crucifixion is the centerpiece of Christian faith and doctrine, some find the brutality of the cross inconsistent with their image of a loving God and their desire for a gentler, more approachable faith. As a result, some Christians have marginalized the cross or fundamentally reinterpreted it to downplay or remove any aspect of God's judgment and the brutality of Jesus's death. Are they right? Would a cross-less Christianity be more loving and less violent and have wider appeal?

This cross-less perspective is appealing only if we hold a narrow, one-dimensional view of the cross. If we assume that Jesus's self-sacrifice was necessary for the forgiveness of sins and nothing more, we may naturally ask, "Why couldn't God just forgive us without the cross? After all, the Bible is loaded with examples of God forgiving people without the need for a blood sacrifice." What this view ignores, however, is that the cross is more than an instrument of forgiveness.

To be clear, the cross *is* where Jesus died for the sins of the world, but the cross is also God's instrument of justice. As Miroslav Volf says, "The cross is not forgiveness pure and simple, but God's setting aright the world of injustice and deception."[2] Through the cross, God judged the world's evil by revealing the magnitude of its horror and ugliness. Before it reconciled us to God through the forgiveness of our sins, the cross first told us the truth about our sins.

Imagine Christianity without the cross. In cross-less Christianity, a term originating with German theologian Dietrich Bonhoeffer,[3] God simply forgives and forgets without ever exposing the true ugliness of our evil and condemning it. Without the cross, we are never confronted by the real magnitude of our injustice or the extravagance of God's love that redeemed us from it. A cross-less faith would be constructed on what Bonhoeffer calls "cheap grace."[4] If forgiveness could be obtained at no cost, then our offenses really weren't that terrible to begin with. Such cheap

WHAT IF JESUS WAS SERIOUS ABOUT JUSTICE?

grace might bring comfort to villains, but it would only compound the suffering of their victims. Without the cross, God would be declaring that atrocities like murder, rape, genocide, slavery, and all kinds of dehumanizing oppression are no big deal, that forgiveness is easy, and that the horrors experienced by the victims of injustice aren't so bad. A cross-less Christianity does not take evil—in the world or in us—seriously.

For God to be truly good, he must acknowledge the full gravity of evil and oppose it in every form. Again, Volf writes, "A nonindignant God would be an accomplice in injustice, deception, and violence."[5] With the cross, God isn't merely forgiving the world's evil; he is showing how truly terrible our evil is. This reality is what makes the cross so powerful and unique among religions. According to the New Testament, the cross of Christ is *simultaneously* the device of God's judgment against evil *and* the instrument of his mercy toward those who've committed it.

 READ MORE: John 12:27–36; Romans 3:21–26

34 IF JESUS WAS SERIOUS . . . THEN IN WHAT WAY DID GOD FORSAKE HIM ON THE CROSS?

SOME CONTEMPORARY CHRISTIANS resist the notion that divine wrath played a role at the cross, fearing that this notion casts God as a moral monster who tortured his own innocent Son. But one faithful solution preserves the biblical testimony that Jesus is the "atoning sacrifice for our sins" (1 John 4:10) without making the Father into a cosmic child abuser. This solution requires understanding the cross through the lens of passive wrath.

In a previous chapter, we explored the two sides of God's wrath. First is his active wrath—God's exceedingly rare, direct punishment of evil and its perpetrators. Second is the far more common dynamic of passive wrath—God stepping aside and allowing people to experience the natural consequences of their own evil decisions. Paul repeatedly says that sinful people experienced divine wrath when God turned away and "gave them over" to their desires (Rom. 1:24, 26, 28). This is the language of passive wrath, and it's used by Jesus himself on the cross.

Shortly before Jesus dies, he quotes Psalm 22:1: "My God, my God, why have you forsaken me?" (Matt. 27:46; Mark 15:34). The exact theological meaning and significance of Jesus's cry have been debated for two millennia. There is space for multiple interpretations, but one in particular intrigues me. Being "forsaken" by God seems inconsistent with any understanding of active wrath. No one being assaulted would shout at their attacker, "Why are you ignoring me?!" That's ridiculous because we cannot actively engage *and* forsake someone at the same time.

Instead, Jesus's perception that God the Father had turned away from him is consistent with the biblical idea of passive wrath. God's people are forsaken and his wrath is revealed when he removes his hand of protection, turns away, and allows them to experience the bitter fruit of their own evil desires and behavior.

In its original context, Psalm 22 is not about God's active punishment. It's about God's apparent failure to rescue David from the evils that surround him. I think Jesus, on the cross, used David's words the same way. He did not experience the Father's active wrath on the cross, as some Christian traditions emphasize. Rather, Jesus experienced what happens when the Father turns aside, hands one over to the forces of evil, and allows the world to do its worst. Biblically speaking, this forsaking of God the Son was a manifestation of God's wrath—just not the active sort we normally assume.

In no way should this interpretation diminish our vision of Jesus's suffering. Here's one way to think about it. Although the consequences of human evil have been evident ever since we rebelled against God in the garden of Eden, what if God had mercifully prevented humanity from experiencing most of the natural consequences of our evil? Like a levee holding back the sea, what if God had sheltered humanity from the worst of its own injustice? What if he had waited until his own Son was on the cross to turn away, to remove his hand, and to allow the levee to break so that the tsunami of human evil—the accumulated consequences of all our past, present, and future sins—crashed upon Jesus rather than us? Could that be the unimaginable pain that provoked Jesus's cry of abandonment?

In this view, it is still God's wrath that is revealed through the cross. But rather than God the Father actively torturing his innocent Son, as some traditions have preached, it's the wrath of God in the form of the world's evil that is allowed to overwhelm and consume Jesus. God the Son is the innocent victim of all the forces of evil since the beginning of time. He reaped the bitter harvest of pain that humanity deserved. He suffered the consequences of our sins. As Isaiah 53:5–6 puts it:

> But he was pierced for our transgressions,
>   he was crushed for our iniquities;
> the punishment that brought us peace was on him,
>   and by his wounds we are healed.
> We all, like sheep, have gone astray,
>   each of us has turned to our own way;
> and the LORD has laid on him
>   the iniquity of us all.

Far from a moral monster causing the suffering of his beloved Son, God the Father shares in the grief and agony as he witnesses the full horrors of the world's evil at the cross. In other words, rather than seeing God the Son as the innocent victim and God the Father as the angry villain, we recognize that both the Son and the Father experienced pain as they together accomplished the salvation of the world. This is why, rather than pitting one member of the Trinity against another, Paul can declare that "God was reconciling the world to himself in Christ, not counting people's sins against them" (2 Cor. 5:19).

 READ MORE: Matthew 27:45–50; 1 John 4:7–21

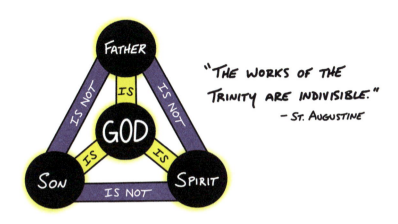

35. IF JESUS WAS SERIOUS... THEN THE CROSS IS PRIMARILY ABOUT GOD'S LOVE

SCRIPTURE SPEAKS ABOUT JESUS paying the penalty for the world's sins through his death on the cross—a doctrine known as penal substitutionary atonement. *Penal* means "punishment." *Substitutionary* means "to take another's place." And *atonement* means "to repay a debt" or "to reconcile." Therefore, penal substitutionary atonement refers to Jesus receiving the punishment for our sins so that we may be reconciled to God. This, the Bible says, is part of what Jesus accomplished through his death on the cross. He received the penalty and paid the debt for our evil.

Advocates of this doctrine find plenty of support in Scripture. Isaiah prophesies that the Messiah will be "pierced for our transgressions" and "crushed for our iniquities" (Isa. 53:5). John calls Jesus the "atoning sacrifice," or payment, for the sins of the whole world (1 John 2:2). And even Jesus says that he came to "give his life as a ransom for many" (Mark 10:45). Some traditions are so committed to the doctrine of penal substitution that they see it as the entirety of the gospel.

The doctrine, however, also has its critics. They point out that penal substitution, a very legal and judicial framing of the cross, does not capture how the earliest Christians understood Jesus's death. In fact, they note, penal substitutionary atonement was absent from the first millennium of church history and gained wide acceptance only with the Protestant Reformation, starting in the sixteenth century.[1] More importantly, some object to penal substitution on the grounds that it fundamentally changes the gospel from a message about God's love to one about God's anger. The most famous verse in the Bible, John 3:16, says, "God so loved the world that he gave his one and only Son." If penal substitution is to be believed, its critics say, then the verse should say, "God so *hated* the world that he *killed* his one and only Son." Some have even rejected penal substitution because, they say, it amounts to "cosmic child abuse."[2]

So who's right? Is penal substitution the essential heart of the gospel, or is it a wicked perversion? Well, it depends on how exactly one defines the doctrine.

To begin, let's address an error that those on both sides of the debate commit. Some advocates of penal substitution teach that God the Father directly and brutally tortured God the Son on the cross. In their view, the crucifixion was the scene of God's *active* wrath against sin.[3] This is a popular trope in some evangelistic preaching. You may have heard something like "Because of your sin, God's anger and wrath were going to destroy you. But on the cross, Jesus stepped in the way and took the hit from God on your behalf."

If this is someone's view of penal substitutionary atonement, then it's understandable why they might reject it as cosmic child abuse. Rather than a loving Savior, God sounds more like an indiscriminate and unmerciful monster. N. T. Wright refers to this misrepresentation of penal substitution as a "paganization" of the gospel because it fundamentally misunderstands the God of Scripture.[4] It reduces him to a deity who demands blood sacrifices to appease his uncontrollable rage. He doesn't ultimately care who suffers his wrath as long as he gets his pound of flesh.

Of course, that is not what Scripture teaches.

As we saw in the previous chapter, God the Father did not actively torture Jesus on the cross. Instead, he turned away from Jesus and handed him over to the evil powers and dark forces of the world ("My God, my God, why have you forsaken me?" [Ps. 22:1; Matt. 27:46]). In this way, Jesus took upon himself the terrible consequences for our sins, but those consequences were inflicted by the powers of evil and chaos, not by our heavenly Father. So while the cross still represents God's *passive* wrath against sin, the accusation that penal substitution implies cosmic child abuse does not hold.

What's more, the paganized view of penal substitutionary atonement says that God the Father is the executioner and God the Son is his passive target. Again, that is not what Scripture teaches. Instead, the Bible affirms that God's plan to redeem the world through the cross was the work of the Trinity—Father, Son, and Spirit. In other words, Jesus was not an unwilling victim of the Father's plan. It was *Jesus's* plan as well.

Augustine says, "The works of the Trinity are indivisible."[5] And an orthodox view of the Trinity, as affirmed by Gregory of Nyssa, recognizes, "All that the Father is, we see revealed in the Son."[6] In other words, the cross is God taking the punishment for the world's sin upon *himself*. It's a beautiful act of self-sacrifice, not the abuse of a subordinate.

Ultimately, I find many of the arguments for and against penal substitution—which are surprisingly divisive—deeply flawed and often misguided. Isaiah 53:6 states that "the LORD has laid on him the iniquity of us all" (penal), and the Bible repeatedly affirms that Jesus died for our sins (substitution) so that we might

VICTORY AND DEFEAT

be reconciled to God (atonement). The problem occurs when this good, true, and beautiful doctrine gets twisted and changes God from a loving Father into an angry monster.

 READ MORE: John 10:7–18; Colossians 1:15–20

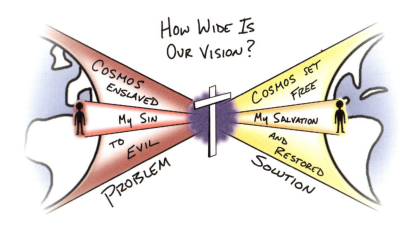

36 IF JESUS WAS SERIOUS . . . THEN HE DID NOT THINK OF ME "ABOVE ALL"

WHAT DID JESUS ACTUALLY ACCOMPLISH on the cross? We know that the Roman and Jewish officials *thought* they had executed a meddlesome revolutionary from Galilee. However, the Gospel writers have a far deeper—even cosmic—interpretation of Jesus's death. The New Testament's understanding of the cross even surpasses what many contemporary Christians have been taught about its power.

WHAT IF JESUS WAS SERIOUS ABOUT JUSTICE?

One popular worship song about Jesus's death includes the lyric "You [Jesus] took the fall and thought of me above all."[1] While Scripture certainly affirms that God's love for us was revealed by Christ's willingness to die for sinners (Rom. 5:8), did he really think of *me* as an individual "above all"?

The Bible reveals that the scope of Jesus's achievement on the cross goes far beyond the redemption of individual sinners. He died not merely for me or even for humanity but to redeem all of creation. Through his death, Jesus Christ triumphed over every enemy, ruler, power, and authority, and all things have been put in subjection under him. Theologians refer to the cosmic scope of Jesus's redemption as *Christus Victor*—Latin for "the victory of Christ." The message of the New Testament is that through his death on the cross, Jesus disarmed and defeated every power of evil, and he is now the rightful King over the entire cosmos. Through the cross, justice has come and every false ruler has been dethroned.

In other words, the cross isn't merely how God rescued me from sin; it's how he rescued the entire cosmos from evil, disorder, and chaos. And rather than thinking about me above other people and things, Christ appeared to be thinking about his own glory and exaltation—his enthronement over all things. As the writer of Hebrews says, Jesus endured the cross "for the joy set before him . . . , scorning its shame, and sat down at the right hand of the throne of God" (12:2). So it appears the individualistic, even self-centered vision of the cross popular in consumer Christianity gets a few things wrong.

Why does this matter? Because what we believe about the scope of Jesus's redemption affects the scope of our Christian lives. If the cross was just about *my* redemption, then the call to follow Christ will be severely limited in our imaginations. It becomes natural, even necessary, to narrowly apply the cross to *my* salvation, *my* life, *my* relationships, and *my* circumstances. This understanding of the Christian's calling leaves little room for any social implications of the cross or for the kind of redemptive justice that reorders the entire world.

If the cross was about Jesus defeating all evil and reigning over all things, as Scripture says, then following Jesus is certainly about submitting my personal life to his reign. But it's also about carrying the healing power of Christ and the justice of his kingdom into every part of the world, including the social, the economic, the political, the physical, and the intellectual. It's about seeing his will done *everywhere* on earth as it is in heaven. As Abraham Kuyper said, "There is not a square inch in the whole domain of our human existence over which Christ, who is Sovereign over all, does not cry, Mine!"[2]

READ MORE: 1 Corinthians 15:20–28; Revelation 11:15–17

37 IF JESUS WAS SERIOUS . . . THEN HIS RESURRECTION DID MORE THAN PROVE HIS DIVINE IDENTITY

WE'VE BEEN ASKING what Jesus accomplished through his death and how the cross reveals the justice of God. But we ought to ask the same question about his resurrection. Unfortunately, many common interpretations of Jesus's resurrection often bypass the New Testament in favor of more sentimental notions.

For example, some who consider themselves modern and enlightened reduce the resurrection to a metaphor—a poetic hope that good will triumph over evil. Yet even the apostle Paul—who was neither modern nor enlightened—understood that if Jesus did not literally and physically rise from the dead, then the Christian faith is meaningless (1 Cor. 15:12-19). Others see the resurrection as verification of Jesus's divine identity. This view says the resurrection doesn't really add anything vital or new to the Gospel accounts of Jesus's life. After all, his messianic identity had already been established before he died. Therefore, the resurrection is just the Gospel writers' way of underlining Jesus's divine nature by ending their stories with an exclamation point.

I heard this resurrection-as-identity-verification view frequently as a teenager in the 1990s, but I later came to see that it misses the resurrection's larger significance. It's like saying the purpose of the Apollo 11 mission was to prove the moon was really there. Yes, it accomplished that, but the reality of the moon was never in doubt. Likewise, Jesus's resurrection *did* validate his identity, but it did much more.

The New Testament writers understood that Jesus's death and resurrection represented a complete and literal triumph over evil. N. T. Wright says it this way:

VICTORY AND DEFEAT

Jesus on the cross towers over the whole scene . . . as the point where the evil of the world does all it can and where the Creator of the world does all that he can. Jesus suffers the full consequences of evil: evil from the political, social, cultural, personal, moral, religious and spiritual angles all rolled into one; evil in the downward spiral hurtling toward the pit of destruction and despair. And he does so precisely as the act of redemption, of taking the downward fall and exhausting it, so that there may be new creation, new covenant, forgiveness, freedom and hope.[1]

The resurrection showed that evil's power, which is epitomized by the permanence of death, had been spent. Evil pushed in all of its chips at the cross; it bet everything on destroying Christ. Evil put every particle of its power into one final knockout punch that landed Jesus in the grave. And by all appearances, it seemed to have worked.

But when Jesus rose from the grave, he showed that evil's power was broken. By taking upon himself all of its darkness on Friday, there was nothing left to keep him in the tomb by Sunday. Far more than just a sentimental hope or even a validation of Jesus's identity, the resurrection revealed that the redemptive justice of God had shattered the curse of sin over his world. The resurrection meant evil's reign was finished and Christ's reign had begun. The order God had intended from the beginning of creation had been restored.

 READ MORE: Colossians 2:13–15; Hebrews 2:14–15

38 IF JESUS WAS SERIOUS . . . THEN THE POWER OF THE CROSS IS STILL WORKING TODAY

WE'VE SEEN HOW JESUS'S UNDERSTANDING of justice was rooted in the Old Testament's stories and laws. Therefore, we shouldn't be surprised to discover that the New Testament accounts draw heavily from the Old Testament story of the exodus to explain the cross. Just as the Lord's justice condemned the evil of Egypt and delivered his people from slavery, through the cross God's justice condemned the evil of the world and delivered his people from slavery to sin.

Jesus makes this link between the exodus and the cross explicit at the meal he shares with his disciples the night before his death. In the Torah, God commanded his people to celebrate the Passover meal each year to remember their deliverance from Egypt. While sharing the meal with his friends, Jesus uses the wine and bread to represent his broken body and shed blood, and he commands them—and all of his followers—to share a communal meal to remember his death on the cross. Many churches quote Jesus's words to his disciples from that meal: "Do this in remembrance of me" (Luke 22:19).

Today, many of us think of remembrance as a mental activity, a recollection of a past event. Therefore, some Christian traditions reduce the bread and the cup to symbols to jog our memories. But in Jesus's culture, remembering had a much richer meaning. It meant becoming an active participant in the past event that is being remembered and inviting all the power of that event into the present. The Passover meal, therefore, wasn't simply about recalling what God did long ago in Egypt; it was also about recognizing how his justice is at work in the world right now. Likewise, at the communion table, we invite the reality of Jesus's salvation—the liberating power of his cross—to free us once again. We gather at his table to remember that God still saves, still liberates, still disarms evil, and still sets his children free.

Evidence that God's power of deliverance is still at work in the world is found in Andrew Young's book about the civil rights movement. He tells about a march on Easter Sunday in Birmingham, Alabama, in 1964. Five thousand people were dressed in their Sunday best ready to march from New Pilgrim Baptist Church to the jail where Martin Luther King Jr. was being held. Everything began peacefully, but then Bull Connor's police force arrived with guns and dogs, and firefighters with hoses blocked the street. The marchers stopped. Young writes:

> Wyatt Walker and I were leading the march. I can't say we knew what to do. I know I didn't want to turn the march around.... I asked people to get down on their knees and offer a prayer.... Suddenly Rev. Charles Billups, one of the most faithful and fearless leaders of the old Alabama Christian Movement for Human Rights, jumped up and hollered, *"The Lord is with this movement! Off your knees! We're going on!"* ... Stunned at first, Bull Connor yelled, "Stop 'em, stop 'em!" But none of the police moved a muscle.... Even the police dogs that had been growling and straining at their leashes... were now perfectly calm.... I saw one fireman, tears in his eyes, just let the hose drop at his feet. Our people marched right between the red fire trucks, singing, "I want Jesus to walk with me." ...
>
> [Bull Connor's] policemen had refused to arrest us, his firemen had refused to hose us, and his dogs had refused to bite us. It was quite a moment to witness. I'll never forget one old woman who became ecstatic when she marched through the barricades. As she passed through, she shouted, "Great God Almighty done parted the Red Sea one mo' time!"[1]

WHAT IF JESUS WAS SERIOUS ABOUT JUSTICE?

That story and many more remind us that God's justice and his power to deliver his people were seen in the Old Testament, they were seen at the cross, and they can still be seen today.

 READ MORE: Exodus 14:10–14; Ephesians 6:10–20

PART 5

REWARD *AND* PUNISHMENT

MATTHEW 25:37–46

Then the righteous will answer him, "Lord, when did we see you hungry and feed you, or thirsty and give you something to drink? When did we see you a stranger and invite you in, or needing clothes and clothe you? When did we see you sick or in prison and go to visit you?"

The King will reply, "Truly I tell you, whatever you did for one of the least of these brothers and sisters of mine, you did for me."

Then he will say to those on his left, "Depart from me, you who are cursed, into the eternal fire prepared for the devil and his angels. For I was hungry and you gave me nothing to eat, I was thirsty and you gave me nothing to drink, I was a stranger and you did not invite me in, I needed clothes and you did not clothe me, I was sick and in prison and you did not look after me."

They also will answer, "Lord, when did we see you hungry or thirsty or a stranger or needing clothes or sick or in prison, and did not help you?"

He will reply, "Truly I tell you, whatever you did not do for one of the least of these, you did not do for me."

Then they will go away to eternal punishment, but the righteous to eternal life.

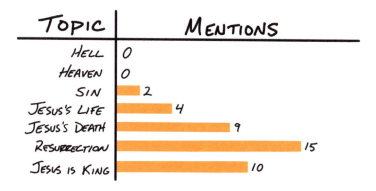

39 IF JESUS WAS SERIOUS... THEN GOD'S JUDGMENT IS NOT THE SAME AS HELL

IN MY PREVIOUS BOOK IN THIS SERIES, I explore how profoundly we've misunderstood what Jesus said about heaven—or, more accurately, "the heavens."[1] The assumption that the kingdom of heaven is a celestial paradise inhabited by the disembodied souls of the righteous after death (rather than the present reality of God's reign here on earth) has caused us to fundamentally misunderstand both Christ's mission and our calling as his people.

Our assumptions about the other place tend to be unbiblical too. In my experience, hell may be the most misunderstood and misapplied element of Christian doctrine. It is the most dangerous kind of idea—one that everyone assumes they understand but few have actually studied, like taxes or Italian cooking. Even those who've never darkened the doors of a church or opened a Bible carry surprisingly detailed ideas about hell. Our history and culture are awash with depictions of devils torturing souls in a subterranean furnace, but are those images rooted in Scripture or merely tradition? And do they jibe with what the Old Testament and Jesus say about God's justice?

I realize this is a sensitive subject; it is one that has split churches, ousted pastors, and stirred controversy. But it's also essential for understanding divine justice. After all, if God is on a mission to restore order and flourishing to his creation, then we need to understand what he plans to do with those who refuse to participate in that work and have dedicated themselves to disorder and evil instead.

As we begin to explore the topic of hell, we must keep the Bible's emphasis on God's judgment of evil in mind, especially what God says about his own character. Very often a dismissive attitude about divine judgment is linked to nonbelief in hell. Conversely, those who emphasize God's judgment often fixate on the horrors of hell—sometimes in high definition. Both, I believe, are inconsistent with the words of Jesus.

For example, the book of Acts contains seven or eight gospel sermons or summaries of the gospel preached by Jesus's apostles. And yet hell is never mentioned in Acts. Not once.[2] If you come from a Christian community that always links the gospel with escaping the fires of hell and whose evangelistic preaching employs terrifying threats of eternal torture, then the complete absence of hell from the preaching of the apostles presents a real problem.

The apostles' silence about hell, however, does not mean Jesus's first followers didn't believe in God's wrath against evil. Divine judgment is explicitly mentioned three times in Acts. Unlike our post-Christian culture with its message of "You be you" even if you are engaged in oppression, injustice, and evil, the apostles *did* recognize the reality of God's judgment and warned people to repent—that is, to go in a new direction. However, unlike some popular expressions of Christianity, the apostles did *not* link God's judgment of evil with an agonizing afterlife in hell. The coming judgment of God and the establishment of justice were part of their gospel preaching, but hell was not.

What does that absence of hell in their preaching mean? If we are to use the teachings of Jesus and his apostles as our guide, then we must avoid bundling divine judgment, wrath, and hell into a single take-it-or-leave-it doctrinal package. Instead, we ought to take our guidance from Scripture, which speaks clearly about

WHAT IF JESUS WAS SERIOUS ABOUT JUSTICE?

God's judgment of evil but much less clearly—and less frequently—about hell. We have already seen that dismissing judgment and wrath because of our culture's discomfort with these doctrines is not faithful to the Bible, but overemphasizing a medieval caricature of hell that is not found in the Bible is equally unfaithful.

READ MORE: Matthew 10:26–31; Acts 17:22–31

40   IF JESUS WAS SERIOUS . . . THEN NOT EVERYONE WILL EXPERIENCE ETERNAL LIFE WITH GOD

BACK IN 1940, C. S. Lewis first wrote about the doctrine of condemnation in his book *The Problem of Pain* and expressed a tension many contemporary Christians still feel. Lewis said, "There is no doctrine which I would more willingly remove from Christianity than this, if it lay in my power. But it has the full support of Scripture and, specially, of Our Lord's own words; it has always been held by Christendom; and it has the support of reason. If a game is played, it must be possible to lose it."[1] Lewis didn't like the idea of hell, but he couldn't just wish it away.

Of course, that hasn't stopped many Christians from trying. Some flatly deny the existence of any hell, but those who hold the Bible and church history with some regard can't be so bold. Instead, they find some clever way to diminish any concern with hell. Several years ago, for example, a Lutheran bishop was asked, "Is there a hell?" She responded, "There may be, but I think it's empty."[2] When asked to justify her view from the Bible, she cited John 12:32, where Jesus says he will be lifted up and draw all people to himself. The bishop understood this to mean that everyone—despite their complicity with evil or their rejection of God—will be compelled to live eternally with him anyway.

This view, that no one will be condemned for eternity, is known as *universalism*. It emphasizes that Jesus's sacrificial death atoned for the world's sins and that, therefore, everyone—whether or not they have repented of their sins and put their trust in Christ—has been rescued from hell and death to enjoy eternity with God. In other words, salvation is universal. Like most doctrines, universalism comes in a number of trims. Some forms erase human agency entirely by imposing reconciliation with God on every individual, whether they want it or not. Other variations are more subtle and argue that a person may persist in their rebellion and separation from God in the afterlife, but because his mercy is limitless, they will have unlimited chances to change their mind and accept his love—and eventually everyone will.

Of course, the doctrine has many more nuances, but they all share a common appeal. Universalism minimizes or eliminates the unpopular Christian concepts of divine judgment, wrath, and punishment to present a vision of God as all-merciful, even toward those who don't want his mercy or who appear fully dedicated to injustice. As we have already explored in previous chapters, both God's justice and his love necessitate the judgment of evil. And the fact that universalism was an extremely uncommon view before the nineteenth century should give us pause. It's a hint that confirmation bias may be involved and that we've departed from the message of Jesus that has been enthusiastically embraced by the global and historic church. Of course, simply because a doctrine is old or popular does not mean it is correct. Ultimately, we must investigate what Scripture says.

Advocates of universalism correctly point out that Scripture says God desires all to be saved (1 Tim. 2:4) and for no one to perish (2 Pet. 3:9). From these texts and others, universalists conclude that God has both the desire and the power to rescue everyone; therefore, he certainly will.

What this argument overlooks is the overwhelming testimony of both Jesus and the apostles that "eternal punishment" will be the fate of those who reject God's love and mercy. The message of the New Testament is not "Everyone's going to be okay; it's just going to take a bit longer for some people to get with the program." Such a message contradicts the urgency and compassion that motivated Jesus's ministry. The same urgency was exhibited by the earliest Christians who carried his ministry forward and suffered as a result.

If everyone's already okay, why bother proclaiming the gospel and risking persecution or death? Universalism just doesn't square with the sacrifices made by the apostles in the New Testament, the persecution endured by the earliest believers in the Roman Empire, or the martyrdom of countless Christians throughout the centuries.

Likewise, while people who espouse universalism may want to elevate human value by eliminating hell, many versions of the doctrine inadvertently diminish human value by eliminating human agency. This view forces every individual to surrender to God's love, whether they want to or not. Can such a coercive posture by God still be considered loving? Many theological traditions say no.

Universalism must overlook the reality that some people continually and actively reject Christ's offer of love and forgiveness. This is what Lewis means when he says, "If a game is played, it must be possible to lose it." He understands that some people will reject God's definition of justice because it will not allow them to remain in ultimate control, and such people don't want God and

REWARD AND PUNISHMENT

never will. Respecting their agency, God will sorrowfully grant them their broken desire. This is why Lewis concludes that hell is a necessary outcome of human free will: "I willingly believe that the damned are, in one sense, successful rebels to the end; the gates of hell are locked from the inside."[3]

 READ MORE: John 12:44–50; 2 Peter 3:8–10

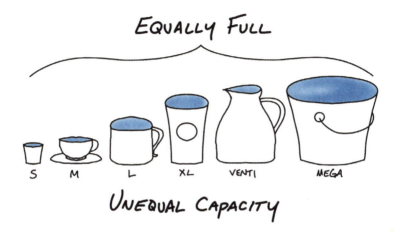

41 IF JESUS WAS SERIOUS . . . THEN NOT EVERYONE WILL RECEIVE THE SAME REWARD OR PUNISHMENT

HUMAN JUSTICE, as flawed as it is, is guided by the principle of proportionality. Simply put, we recognize that the punishment should fit the crime. That is why we do not impose the same penalty for every offense. A child lying to their mother is different from a witness lying in court. Both are wrong, but only one is criminal. And even within the category of criminal law, not all crimes incur the same penalty. It is right and just for murder to be punished more severely than money laundering, and for a terrorist to face a greater penalty than a thief.

Everyone intuitively understands that justice, by definition, must be proportional. Our human justice systems employ this principle imperfectly, but God's justice does so with perfection. The Bible clearly says, "God will repay each person according to what they have done" (Rom. 2:6; see also Ps. 62:12; Prov. 24:12). In these passages, proportionality is applied to both the righteous and the wicked. In other words, divine justice means not everyone will receive the same reward and not everyone will receive the same punishment.

For example, in 1 Corinthians, the apostle Paul writes about the evaluation that awaits followers of Jesus. He says the quality of each person's work will be revealed with fire on the day of judgment. Employing a construction metaphor, Paul says, "If anyone builds on this foundation using gold, silver, costly stones, wood, hay or straw, their work will be shown for what it is" (3:12–13). A reward awaits those whose work endures the testing, but if it's consumed by the fire, "the builder will suffer loss but yet will be saved—even though only as one escaping through the flames" (3:15).

With this metaphor, Paul is echoing a theme found throughout the Bible and one Jesus speaks about frequently: God rewards his people relative to their good works. But like so many other aspects of divine justice, proportionality has fallen out of favor with some modern Christians. The notion that in God's kingdom some people will experience greater rewards than others violates our cultural expectation of equity. We've been shaped to believe that a redeemed and perfected world cannot include any hierarchy of status or difference in outcome. Everyone, we assume, will be equal in every way in God's kingdom, but neither Jesus nor his apostles teach this.

In fact, Jesus speaks often about rewarding his disciples for their good works. For example, he says that anyone who gives even a cup of cold water "will certainly not lose their reward" (Matt. 10:42). And the Bible ends with a warning from Jesus, emphasizing that he will judge and reward proportionally. "Look, I am coming soon! My reward is with me, and I will give to each person *according to what they have done*" (Rev. 22:12).

What does it mean for Christ's people to experience different rewards in the age to come? I appreciate how Jonathan Edwards imagines it. He compares heavenly rewards to cups of different sizes. "Every vessel that is cast into this ocean of happiness is full, though there are some vessels far larger than others."[1] In other words, everyone will be "filled to the measure of all the fullness of God," as Paul says (Eph. 3:19). According to Edwards, then, "there shall be no such thing as envy in heaven."[2] No one will lack, but some will be rewarded with a greater capacity to experience God's fullness than others. Like so much about the renewed creation, this is only a metaphor of a reality we cannot fully comprehend this side of glory.

This biblical principle of proportionality doesn't just apply to rewards. It also guides God's judgment of evil. Both the Old and the New Testaments affirm God's vengeance against the wicked as proportional. "It is mine to avenge; I will repay," says the Lord (Deut. 32:35; Rom. 12:19). And Jesus also alludes to different degrees of punishment for the wicked, with some experiencing far more loss than others based on the gravity of their evil deeds (see Matt. 11:24).

Why does this matter? Erasing or ignoring the biblical understanding of proportional justice results in two errors. First, it risks producing lackadaisical disciples. Too many of us Christians assume that the pursuit of good works is nonessential to our calling because we have a ticket into paradise. If we're already counted among the "sheep," then what's the point in doing anything more? While Scripture is clear that we cannot earn our place with God through our good works, we are nonetheless created and redeemed in Christ Jesus "to do good works" (Eph. 2:8–10).

Second, without a vision of proportionality, pop Christianity presents a false vision of God that is understandably odious to people outside the faith. If the same punishment awaits everyone who rejects life with God, regardless of how much misery and evil they caused, how can the Christian God be considered good?

REWARD AND PUNISHMENT

Without proportionality, God's justice appears more unfair and flawed than human justice, and that is precisely the opposite of what Jesus teaches.

READ MORE: Matthew 11:20–24; James 1:12–15

GEHENNA [GI-HEN-UH] NOUN
1. THE VALLEY NEAR JERUSALEM WHERE SACRIFICES TO IDOLS WERE MADE THAT LATER BECAME THE CITY'S GARBAGE DUMP. } WHAT'S COMFORTABLE
2. THE REALM WHERE GOD WILL PUNISH & DESTROY EVIL.
SYNONYM: HELL

} WHAT JESUS MEANT

42 IF JESUS WAS SERIOUS . . . THEN HELL ISN'T JUST A PLACE ON EARTH

GEHENNA IS THE GREEK WORD most commonly translated as "hell" in our English Bibles, and it wasn't just a theological idea. It was an actual place familiar to everyone Jesus spoke to in first-century Judea. Gehenna was a narrow valley south of Jerusalem that later served as the city's garbage dump, and it was long associated with evil. This valley was where idolatrous Jews generations earlier had sacrificed their children to the pagan god Molech and where later generations disposed of the bodies of those believed to be cursed by God: criminals, sinners, and rebels. Gehenna was where worthless things were cast out to be destroyed, and to consume the city's never-ending waste, a fire burned in the valley day and night.

Unfortunately, this connection between hell, *gehenna*, and Jerusalem's city dump has been exaggerated by some Bible teachers as a way to diminish or ignore everything Jesus said about hell. Because Gehenna was the name of an actual geographic location, some have argued that Jesus had only this valley in mind when he spoke about hell and that his listeners would have understood that he was talking about the garbage pit outside Jerusalem, *not* a place of divine judgment for the wicked after death. However, this argument has two significant flaws.

First, a belief that God would judge and repay evildoers for their wickedness after death was widely held among first-century Jews. Jesus and his disciples did not invent the idea of hell. It was common within their culture already (with the exception of the Sadducees, who did not believe in a resurrection or afterlife for either the righteous or the wicked). For example, one Jewish source from Jesus's time says that on the coming day of judgment, God will "drag [the devil], and his hosts also, into *gehenna*," and after the resurrection of the dead he will "cause fire" to "consume all the impious, and they will become as if they had not been created."[1]

These ideas were very familiar to Jesus's audience. Therefore, when he spoke about *gehenna*, fire, and the destruction of the wicked, they would not have limited their imaginations to the city garbage dump that used the same name. The valley outside Jerusalem was merely a metaphor, a vivid illustration of God's coming judgment of evil and those who practiced it.

Second, the words of Jesus simply don't make sense if he intended his listeners to think of hell/*gehenna* as only the literal trash pit outside the city. In numerous passages, it's clear that Jesus uses the word *gehenna* to refer to a place of divine punishment, not the valley outside Jerusalem.

> Anyone who says, "You fool!" will be in danger of the fire of [*gehenna*]. (Matt. 5:22)

> It is better for you to lose one part of your body than for your whole body to be thrown into [*gehenna*]. (5:29)

> Be afraid of the One who can destroy both soul and body in [*gehenna*]. (10:28)

In all of these verses, *gehenna* clearly references the Jewish belief in a place of divine punishment, not the literal valley south of Jerusalem. So those who say that Jesus spoke not about hell but only about a local garbage dump are not only misreading his words but also ignoring the cultural and religious beliefs of the

WHAT IF JESUS WAS SERIOUS ABOUT JUSTICE?

audience who received them. The right question is not, Did Jesus speak about hell? (because he certainly did) but rather, *What* did Jesus say about hell, and does it match the traditional vision of hell that's been widely accepted?

READ MORE: Matthew 5:21–26; 10:26–42

43 IF JESUS WAS SERIOUS . . . THEN GOD'S JUSTICE IS UNDYING, BUT THOSE WHO FACE IT ARE NOT

SO FAR WE'VE SEEN the errors made by those who wish to minimize hell or eliminate it from Christianity. The view that everyone will ultimately live forever with God, known as universalism, does not fit with what the Bible says about divine justice or what Jesus says about judgment. Likewise, those who say that *gehenna* refers only to a local garbage dump and not to God's final judgment of the wicked are rejecting what was commonly understood in Jesus's own cultural context.

But the errors about hell are not limited to those seeking to eliminate it. There are also Christians who mistakenly inflate the doctrine of hell beyond what Jesus or his apostles taught. For example, a common view is that the wicked will suffer perpetually in hell for all eternity. Some refer to this as the traditional view of hell because it is very old. Theologians have given it a more descriptive name: eternal conscious torment (ECT).

While we should factor church history and church teachings into our evaluation of any doctrine, tradition alone is not enough to eclipse the words of Jesus or the Bible. Therefore, we need to assess the ECT view of hell in light of Scripture, and that's where things get interesting.

Some Christians, in their eagerness to defend the traditional view of hell, see evidence for ECT in passages of the Bible where none exists. Psychologists call this "motivated reasoning." It's when our biases, both conscious and unconscious, affect how we perceive information.

For example, advocates for the view of hell as never-ending torture often cite Mark 9:43–48 to justify their belief. In this passage, Jesus warns about being thrown into hell, where "the worms that eat them do not die, and the fire is not quenched" (v. 48). Here, Jesus is actually quoting the Old Testament. In Isaiah 66, the Lord describes the fate of the righteous and the wicked. The righteous will live with God in a new heaven and new earth, while all humankind "will go out and look on the dead bodies of those who rebelled against me; the worms that eat them will not die, the fire that burns them will not be quenched, and they will be loathsome to all mankind" (66:24).

If we come to these texts already assuming the traditional view of hell, then we will be predisposed to interpret the undying worms and the unquenchable fire as evidence for eternal torture. For example, one vocal advocate for the never-ending torture doctrine acknowledges that our finite bodies cannot literally burn or be eaten by insects forever. Therefore, his view is that those sent to hell must be given new, imperishable bodies for the fire and the worms to perpetually consume. He writes this about the description of hell in Isaiah 66: "Though not mentioned specifically in this text, this scene *seems to assume* that God's enemies have been given a body fit for an unending punishment."[1]

Is it the biblical text that "seems to assume" unending punishment or the person interpreting it? This is a classic example of motivated reasoning. The interpreter brings their predetermined view of hell (ECT) to Isaiah 66 and therefore assumes the existence of imperishable bodies and eternal torture.

Let's look carefully at what these verses cited by Jesus actually say.

First, these verses give no indication that those being consumed by the worms and the fire are alive or conscious in any way. In fact, Isaiah explicitly says the worms and the fire are consuming the "dead bodies" of the Lord's enemies who had already been judged and killed (see Isa. 66:16, 24). Only those influenced by motivated reasoning could interpret "dead bodies" to really mean "consciously alive people tortured for eternity." But that's precisely what defenders of the traditional view do with these words of Jesus.

Second and very important, in Mark 9, Jesus identifies the worms and the fire of *gehenna*, *not* the people sent there, as undying. Both here and in Isaiah 66, the worms and the fire are the instruments of God's justice against evil. By identifying these metaphorical means of justice as undying and unquenchable, Scripture declares that nothing will extinguish or interrupt God's judgment. Simply put, the undying worms and the unquenchable fire are the Bible's way of saying that *God's justice* is inescapable and eternal. The people who are subject to it are not eternal.

Taken together, Jesus words about hell and the Old Testament passage he references paint a ghastly and terrible image of the death of the wicked and their bodies being dishonored and defiled. Jesus's words would have been clear to his listeners—God's judgment is coming, it's unavoidable, and it is to be taken seriously! Therefore, those who dismiss Jesus's warning about hell are not faithfully interpreting his warning, but neither are those who allow tradition and motivated reasoning to concoct an image of hell that Jesus never intended.

 READ MORE: Isaiah 66:15–24; Mark 9:43–48

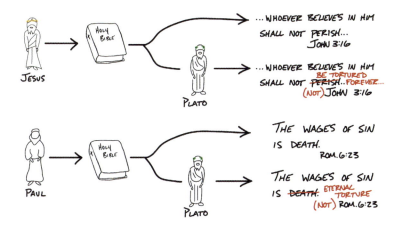

44 IF JESUS WAS SERIOUS . . . THEN NOT EVERY HUMAN SOUL IS IMMORTAL

MANY IN WESTERN SOCIETIES, including many Christians, assume that human beings are immortal creatures. Our bodies may deteriorate with age and eventually die, but our souls are everlasting. Based on this assumption, the most important question anyone could possibly ask is "Where will your soul reside for eternity?" It's a very rational question and one often used to begin a conversation about the gospel or an evangelistic sermon. And it's the reason why so much of the Western church has been preoccupied with heaven and hell.

We've been so thoroughly shaped by this assumption of immortality that most of us blindly carry it into our reading of Scripture. For example, in Genesis, we are told that Adam and Eve were subject to death because of their sin. But how exactly? There are two possibilities. One is that Adam and Eve were created by God as immortal creatures but that their sin contaminated or broke this innate quality, leading to death. The second possibility is that Adam and Eve were created by God as mortal creatures but were given access to immorality, which their sin later blocked.

Consider Genesis 3:22: "The man . . . must not be allowed to reach out his hand and take also from the tree of life and eat, and live forever." This verse implies that the man is mortal but that access to the tree will give him unending life. His sin against God blocks him from the tree, and therefore he remains subject to death. In much of Western Christianity, which assumes all people are intrinsically immortal, this second explanation never enters our imaginations.

Adding to the argument that humans are not inherently immortal are the facts that the ancient Hebrews had no concept of an eternal soul and that nowhere in the Old Testament or the New are all people said to be immortal. So if this belief is not from the Bible, where did it come from?

You can thank the Greek philosopher Plato and other thinkers in the Western classical tradition. Contrary to the Bible, Plato made a strong distinction between the material and the spiritual and argued that every human soul lives on after the body dies. Centuries later, the early Christian writer Tertullian adopted Plato's view. According to Tertullian, "Some things are known even by nature: the immortality of the soul, for instance, is held by many. ... I may use, therefore, the opinion of Plato, when he declares, 'Every soul is immortal.'"[1] In other words, Tertullian *assumed* the immortality of the soul because Plato's ideas were so widely embraced throughout the Roman Empire. He never bothered to examine whether that idea conformed to the teachings of the Bible.

Once the Greek idea of the immortal soul took root in the early church, it began to change the way Christians read the Bible. If all people were immortal and the faithful enjoyed life with God forever, then logic dictated that the wicked must experience the opposite forever as well. As historian Le Roy Froom notes, "It was Tertullian who first affirmed that torments of the lost will be co-equal and co-exist with the happiness of the saved." To reconcile Plato's ideas of the immortal soul and unending torture with the Bible, Tertullian "altered the sense of Scripture and the meaning of words, so as to interpret 'death' as eternal misery and 'destruction' and 'consume' as pain and anguish. 'Hell' became perpetually dying, but never dead."[2]

Why does this matter? Because it reveals that the traditional view of hell as eternal conscious torment is built on a foundation of Greek philosophy rather than biblical theology. And squaring this assumption with Scripture requires redefining what words mean or twisting the plain reading of the Bible. For example, Paul says, "The wages of sin is death" (Rom. 6:23), but that doesn't fit with Plato's view that all human souls are immortal. Therefore, Christians slowly began to redefine "death" throughout the Bible. Romans 6 may say "The wages of sin is death," but some will argue that what Paul *meant* to say was "The wages of sin is never-ending torture."

Likewise, Jesus says, "Do not be afraid of those who kill the body but cannot kill the soul. Rather, be afraid of the One who can destroy both soul and body in hell" (Matt. 10:28). According to those who believe hell is a domain of eternal conscious torture, Jesus didn't really mean that hell is where God destroys bodies and souls, because Plato said human souls can't be destroyed. Therefore, "destroy" should be reinterpreted as "tortured"—which is a very tortured translation, if you'll forgive the pun.

Holding Plato's view of the soul's immortality even warps how we read the most famous verse in the Bible. Jesus says, "For God so loved the world that he gave his one and only Son, that whoever believes in him shall not perish but have eternal life" (John 3:16). The word "perish" was as plainly understood in Jesus's culture as it is in ours. It means to die and the cessation of conscious life. But if no one really perishes, as Plato said, then we must significantly reinterpret John 3:16. According to those holding a traditional

REWARD AND PUNISHMENT

view of hell, God's Son rescues us not from perishing but from never-ending torture.

I could go on with a dozen more verses, but I think you get the point. In our study of God's justice and the doctrine of hell, we must make a choice to give authority to the words of Scripture or the weight of tradition. We must decide whom to take more seriously, Plato or Jesus.

 READ MORE: Genesis 3:17–24; Romans 6:20–23

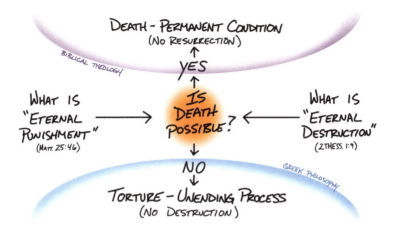

45 IF JESUS WAS SERIOUS... THEN "ETERNAL PUNISHMENT" MAY NOT MEAN WHAT YOU THINK

DEATH IS NOT A RECENT INVENTION, nor is it culturally defined. The ancient Jews, Greeks, and Romans understood death the same way we do. Death is the cessation of life, the end of existence. Therefore, when Jesus speaks about "perishing" (John 3:16) and "dying in your sins" (8:24), and when Paul says that "the wages of sin is death" (Rom. 6:23) and that "if you live according to the flesh, you will die" (8:13), they are simply repeating a consistent and coherent biblical message that goes all the way back to the garden of Eden: the consequence of sin is death, the cessation of life.

Hundreds of passages in the Old and New Testaments reinforce this basic, straightforward message, and yet a significant number of Christians reject it. Rather than accepting that the ultimate fate of those who reject God is death, they say their fate will instead be an eternal life of misery. To reconcile this with what Scripture says, they ignore or downplay many verses, fundamentally redefine what "death" means in others, and exaggerate the few verses that potentially support the eternal conscious torment view of hell.

For example, in Matthew 25:46, Jesus describes the fate of the wicked as "eternal punishment," and Paul says it is "everlasting destruction" in 2 Thessalonians 1:9. If we read these passages while holding to Plato's assumption that all souls are immortal, then we may think the Bible confirms the perpetual agony of the wicked. This view, first introduced to the church by Tertullian in the second century, also benefits from an appealing symmetry. If the saved enjoy eternity in paradise with God, and if all human souls are indestructible, then the damned must consciously suffer for eternity without him. This inference explains why some Christians believe the phrase "eternal punishment" means that the action of being punished will never cease. Likewise, if we hold Plato's assumption that all souls are immortal and therefore cannot be destroyed, then we must interpret "eternal destruction" to mean that the *process* of being destroyed is without end.

But what happens when we hear these passages the way Jesus's culture did, without importing Greek philosophy from Plato? What if we *don't* assume all people are unconditionally and automatically immortal? We may discover that "eternal" refers not to a perpetual *process* but to a permanent *condition*.

For example, if souls can be destroyed, then "eternal destruction" simply means "permanently and irreversibly destroyed." When someone receives a permanent tattoo, the *process* of being tattooed is not unending. Rather, the tattoo itself is everlasting. Likewise, eternal punishment doesn't mean the never-ending process of torture, as many assume. It means the punishment of death itself is permanent, final, and irreversible.

These phrases come into even sharper focus when we read them in the ancient Jewish context in which Jesus preached and Paul wrote. The concept of resurrection was widespread among Jews who believed that the righteous who belonged to God's people would be raised back to life on the coming day of the Lord. So when Jesus speaks of eternal punishment or the destruction of the wicked, he is referring to their eternal condition. The wicked won't be given another chance, nor will they share in the age to come through the resurrection. Unlike those committed to Christ, who are raised to everlasting life, those who reject him remain "dead in [their] transgressions and sins" (Eph. 2:1).

Trying to reconcile Greek ideas about the immortal soul with what Jesus says about judgment creates more problems than it solves and requires a redefinition of words that stretches credulity. Reading these texts in light of Jewish understandings about judgment, death, and resurrection provides a much less convoluted and more straightforward interpretation. While not always the case, very often the simplest reading of a text turns out to be the best one.

 READ MORE: Matthew 25:31–46; 2 Thessalonians 1:5–12

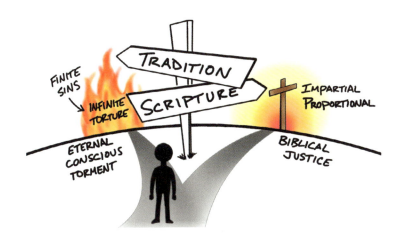

46 IF JESUS WAS SERIOUS... THEN FINITE SINS CANNOT BE PUNISHED WITH INFINITE TORTURE

EARLIER, WE SAW THAT PROPORTIONALITY is an unavoidable and vital aspect of God's coming justice. Throughout the Bible and certainly in Jesus's teachings, we discover that God will "repay" each person based on what they have done—both the wicked and the righteous. But proportionality presents a significant problem for those who say the wicked will live forever in torment.

Humans are finite creatures. We are limited in power, space, and time. Therefore, while we are capable of extraordinary amounts of evil, such evil is still finite. But advocates of the traditional view of hell (known as eternal conscious torment) say that our *finite* sins will be punished with *infinite* torture. To state the obvious, that is *not* proportional—and theologians know it.

Some proponents of eternal conscious torment (ECT) have tried to rebalance the scales of justice by arguing that "to sin against an infinitely glorious being is an infinitely heinous offense that is worthy of an infinitely heinous punishment."[1] In other words, rather than God repaying each person based on what they have done, he will repay each person based on *whom they've done it to*. And because God is infinite, sinning against him incurs infinite suffering. At first glance, this argument might appear logical and fair, but a closer inspection reveals two significant problems.

First, this argument isn't found anywhere in the Bible. We've already explored what the Bible says about the fate of the wicked. It repeatedly says they will be repaid proportionally for their sins and ultimately cease to exist. "The wages of sin is death" (Rom. 6:23). Scripture provides shockingly little support for ECT, but it provides absolutely zero support for the notion that *because the God we've sinned against is eternal, the just consequence for our sins is eternal torture.*

Second, Scripture actively rejects this understanding of justice. One of the great contributions of the Old Testament law is its impartiality. It was common in the ancient world for the powerful to live by one set of rules and the poor by another. But the Lord repeatedly commands his people to apply the law and its consequences equally to the rich and to the poor, to citizens as well as to foreigners. (Deut. 1:16–17; Exod. 23:3, 6; and Lev. 19:15 are just a few of the dozens of verses forbidding favoritism in the law or in the administration of justice.)

In ancient Israel, justice was to be administered equally, regardless of a person's identity. According to the Old Testament, God shows no partiality (see 2 Chron. 19:7). Therefore, he forbids his people from twisting justice based on a person's identity. His law says mistreating an immigrant is not less sinful than mistreating a countryman; similarly, murdering a nobleman is not a greater offense than murdering a servant. Simply put, according to the Bible, the identity of neither the perpetrator nor the victim should define a crime or its consequences.

This biblical commitment to both proportionality and impartiality is why justice is often personified in Western cultures as a blindfolded woman holding balanced scales. In the ECT view of hell, however, the scales are dramatically *un*balanced. Repaying finite sins with infinite torture violates the principle of proportionality. Advocates of this view try to solve this problem by removing justice's blindfold as well. They argue that the punishment should fit not the crime but rather the victim. And because an infinite God is the victim of our sins, we deserve infinite torture.

WHAT IF JESUS WAS SERIOUS ABOUT JUSTICE?

Ironically, this attempt to justify the traditional view of hell requires denying God's own laws. Accepting ECT means ignoring what God says about his own character and what he commands his people to do in their exercise of justice, all in defense of a doctrine about hell that is rooted more in Greek philosophy than in the Bible. Simply put, to defend an unbiblical vision of hell, advocates of ECT must abandon the biblical vision of justice.

 READ MORE: Leviticus 24:17–22; Deuteronomy 1:15–18

47 IF JESUS WAS SERIOUS . . . THEN THE PRICE HE PAID ON THE CROSS WAS DEATH, NOT ETERNAL TORTURE

HUNDREDS OF YEARS BEFORE JESUS WAS BORN, Isaiah prophesied about the meaning of the Messiah's suffering: "But he was pierced for our transgressions, he was crushed for our iniquities; the punishment that brought us peace was on him, and by his wounds we are healed. We all, like sheep, have gone astray, each of us has turned to our own way; and the LORD has laid on him the iniquity of us all" (Isa. 53:5–6).

Isaiah describes how the Messiah will take upon himself the punishment that we deserve. Theologically, this is known as substitutionary atonement. It refers to the debt for a person's sins being paid by someone else on their behalf (see chap. 35 for more). This doctrine is beautifully captured in a well-known hymn called "Jesus Paid It All." The song speaks of the debt caused by our sins and how Jesus took upon himself the complete cost:

> Sin had left a crimson stain,
> He washed it white as snow.

These are ideas and images that fill our songs and our sermons and that we teach to even young children in the church. They are core to the Christian faith.

Substitutionary atonement is very closely linked to another theological concept—*imputation*, which means "to give" or "to ascribe." New Testament scholars, particularly those from the Reformed tradition, sometimes speak of *double imputation*. First, our sins were given to Christ on the cross, and he paid their penalty. Then Christ's righteousness was given to us so that we can stand innocent before God. As Paul says, "God made him who had no sin to be sin for us, so that in him we might become the righteousness of God" (2 Cor. 5:21). Many see these two ideas—substitutionary atonement and double imputation—as essential aspects of Christian doctrine. And I agree!

But these important beliefs raise a question: If Jesus paid it all, what exactly was that payment? Here, the New Testament is crystal clear: Jesus *died* for our sins (1 Cor. 15:1–4). In fact, hundreds of verses contain this same message: through his death on the cross, Jesus received and extinguished the consequences for our sins so that we might be reconciled to God. And this message fits with both the Old and the New Testaments, which speak of death as the effect of sin. We see this as early as Genesis, where God warns the man not to eat from the tree of the knowledge of good and evil, lest he "certainly die" (2:17). And Paul repeats this core biblical idea when he says, "The wages of sin is death" (Rom. 6:23). In other words, the punishment we deserve for our evil and injustice is death, and this is precisely the punishment Jesus accepted on our behalf on the cross.

Here's the problem. Some popular forms of Christianity say the punishment for our sins is not death but rather an eternal existence of never-ending torture. But that is *not* the punishment Jesus experienced for our sins. On this point, even advocates of the eternal torture view agree. Again, the New Testament is clear that Jesus *died* for our sins; he was not eternally tortured for them. For the doctrines of substitutionary atonement and double imputation to work, Jesus had to take upon himself the same penalty we deserve for our sins. He had to pay the debt we owe. These doctrines simply don't work if Jesus paid a different price by accepting a different penalty.

WHAT IF JESUS WAS SERIOUS ABOUT JUSTICE?

So we are left with two choices. Either the penalty for our sins really is *eternal torture*—and we must reject or significantly redefine the doctrines of substitutionary atonement and double imputation—or the penalty for our sins is *death*, as Scripture says, and we can confidently say Jesus paid it all on the cross, give thanks for his substitutionary atonement, and celebrate our redemption from sin, evil, and death. I hope you can see that what's really at stake here isn't merely our understanding of hell but also our understanding of God's justice, the cross, and the gospel itself.

 READ MORE: Romans 5:6–11; 1 Peter 2:21–25

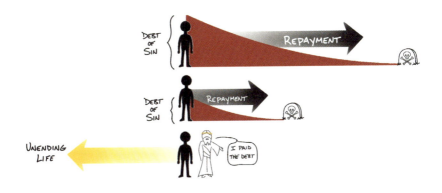

48 IF JESUS WAS SERIOUS . . . THEN THE WICKED WILL FACE DEATH AND WILL PAY FOR THEIR SINS

LET'S SUMMARIZE WHAT WE'VE DISCOVERED SO FAR.
First, Jesus clearly speaks about judgment, hell, and the death of the wicked. So the view that everyone will enjoy eternal life with God is very difficult to sync with Christ's words. Second, the common idea of hell as a place of never-ending torture does not align with the Bible. It ignores or twists the overwhelming number

of passages that speak of death as the consequence for sin, it assumes from Greek philosophy that all souls are immortal, it violates what God declares about his own justice, and it strips Jesus's death on the cross of its substitutionary meaning.

All of this has led some students of the Bible to accept a view known throughout Christian history as *annihilationism*. Although it has variations, annihilationism is the belief that those who reject God's mercy and remain opposed to his gift of life will be destroyed or annihilated. This theology takes seriously and plainly the Bible's many statements about death being the just penalty for sin.

Some critics of annihilationism, however, say that death alone doesn't sufficiently grapple with what Jesus says about proportionality. If everyone who opposes God and practices evil simply dies, if everyone faces the same consequence despite how much harm they have inflicted on others, how are these prospects just? By itself, annihilationism doesn't appear to match what Jesus says about "repaying" each person for what they've done. This shortcoming is why some remain committed to the traditional view of eternal torture despite its many failures.

I believe we must not lose either of the truths Jesus and his apostles taught. On the one hand, death is the ultimate consequence for remaining in sin and rebelling against God's love, but those who give their allegiance to Christ will not perish but have unending life. On the other hand, God's justice is proportional, and each person will be repaid according to what they have done. When these are held together, we get a fuller picture of what divine justice ultimately looks like.

We have already explored how the works of those who belong to Christ will be tested (see chap. 41). Paul says that some will be rewarded and that those whose works are burned up "will suffer loss but yet will be saved—even though only as one escaping through the flames" (1 Cor. 3:15). Here we find that all who give their allegiance to Christ will have eternal life, but not all will experience the same reward. The inverse appears true for those who reject Christ. All of them will die, but not everyone will experience the same punishment before they cease to exist.

It's helpful to note that proportional judgment leading to either eternal life or permanent destruction is not a Christian invention. One Jewish source from the first century speaks about the wicked existing "in darkness and the place of destruction," where they will ultimately "melt away," implying that some might melt toward death more quickly than others.[1]

N. T. Wright seems to have this in mind when he writes, "It is possible for human beings so to continue down this road, so to refuse all whisperings of good news, all glimmers of the true light, all promptings to turn and go the other way, all signposts to the love of God, that after death they become at last, by their own effective choice, *beings that once were human but now are not*, creatures that have ceased to bear the divine image at all."[2]

WHAT IF JESUS WAS SERIOUS ABOUT JUSTICE?

By saying a person can completely lose their human identity and divine image, Wright is using the language of annihilationism. But by speculating that this is a gradual process, he leaves open the possibility that some will endure this loss more slowly and agonizingly than others. In other words, the punishment of being separated from God and life will be mercifully brief for some and a torturously long consequence for others.

 READ MORE: 1 Corinthians 3:12–15; 2 Thessalonians 1:5–10

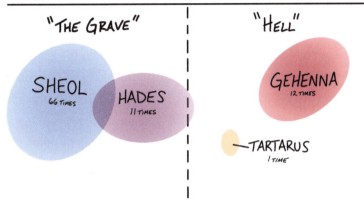

49 IF JESUS WAS SERIOUS . . . THEN HIS PARABLE ABOUT LAZARUS AND THE RICH MAN ISN'T ABOUT HELL

THE BIBLE REPEATEDLY AFFIRMS two things about the fate of those who reject God. First, the Lord, being just, will repay them proportionally for the evil they have done. Second, their final fate, after they've faced the Lord's justice for their wickedness, is death—the cessation of existence. Rather than a realm of unending torture, hell is where evil and those who reject God and his kingdom are ultimately destroyed.

Defenders of hell as a place of never-ending torment often cite a parable of Jesus as evidence for their view. In the parable, found in Luke 16, a poor man named Lazarus is laid near the gate of a rich man who neglects him. Both men die, and Lazarus is carried to Abraham's side, while the rich man experiences torment in Hades. The story proceeds with the rich man begging Abraham for mercy, first for himself, then for his rich and greedy relatives who are still alive and facing the same judgment.

But we ought not build a theology of heaven and hell on this parable. First, Jesus does not tell this story to instruct his disciples about the layout of the afterlife. The reoccurring theme throughout Luke 16 is the dangerous idolatry of money and the foolishness of loving wealth more than God or the poor. The parable of the rich man and Lazarus vividly illustrates this point. To draw any other conclusions is to ignore Jesus's intent. And we must remember that parables are like fables; they are made-up stories to communicate a deeper truth. The characters, settings, and details of a parable are not to be taken literally. As N. T. Wright says, "To take the scene of Abraham, the Rich Man, and Lazarus literally is about as sensible as trying to find out the name of the Prodigal Son."[1]

Second, even those who use the parable as proof of eternal torture are reluctant to take other parts of the story literally. For example, are we to believe Abraham welcomes all who enter paradise like a heavenly Walmart greeter? Will those being tortured in Hades be able to communicate with those in heaven, as the rich man does with Abraham and Lazarus? And will those in paradise constantly look upon the wicked being tortured and hear their cries of agony? Even those flying first class have a privacy curtain to keep us tortured souls in economy out of sight. Is the same courtesy not afforded the righteous in paradise? Again, anyone using this parable as a geographic survey of the afterlife is fundamentally misreading the story.

Third, it's worth noting that Jesus does not identify the rich man's location as *gehenna*, the word usually translated as "hell" in the English Bible. Instead, he uses the Greek word *hadēs*, which, like the Hebrew word *sheol* in the Old Testament, is a generic term for the realm of the dead. In the New Testament, Hades never refers to the final state of the wicked after judgment. In fact, Revelation speaks of Hades giving up the dead to face judgment, after which Hades itself is destroyed (20:13–14). How can the rich man be tortured eternally in a realm that the Bible itself says is temporary?

Fourth and most important, nothing in Jesus's parable indicates that the rich man's agony will never cease. Yes, he is "in torment," and this is understood to be the just consequence for his greed and indifference toward the poor. The rich man experiences the justice of God proportional to the evil of his deeds—a truth affirmed throughout the Bible. But nowhere in the story is his torment described as unending. At the very most, this parable

WHAT IF JESUS WAS SERIOUS ABOUT JUSTICE?

affirms what we have already concluded: the Lord will repay the wicked for their sins. But this story does not provide any evidence that the wicked are immortal or that death is not their final and permanent fate.

 READ MORE: Luke 16:13–14, 19–31

50 IF JESUS WAS SERIOUS . . . THEN THE LAKE OF FIRE IN REVELATION IS ABOUT DESTRUCTION

AN OVERWHELMING AND REPEATED message throughout the Bible is that the wicked will be destroyed. This reality presents a significant and, I believe, insurmountable challenge to the universalist position that all people will ultimately be saved and enjoy eternal life with God. But it also challenges the traditional view of hell as a place of never-ending conscious torment.

WHAT IF JESUS WAS SERIOUS ABOUT JUSTICE?

One book of the Bible that traditionalists cite more than any other is the book of Revelation. Revelation 14:9–11 says that those who worship the beast "will drink the wine of God's fury," they "will be tormented with burning sulfur," and "the smoke of their torment will rise for ever and ever. There will be no rest day or night." This is a graphic warning to those aligned against God and his justice, but does this text outweigh the consistent message of the Psalms, Proverbs, the Prophets, Jesus, and his apostles—namely, that the fate of the wicked is first judgment for their deeds and then ultimately death? Here are some things to consider when reading Revelation 14.

First, the phrase "for ever and ever" may be more literally translated from the original Greek as "for ages upon ages"—meaning "for a very long and indefinite amount of time." Unlike the English idiom "forever and ever," the Greek phrase does not always mean "infinite." The language of smoke "rising forever" was a common Old Testament way of saying that a city's or nation's destruction would be remembered forever and serve as a warning to others (see Isa. 34:9–11).

Second, in another passage, the destruction of Babylon is described using the same phrase. "The smoke from her goes up for ever and ever" (Rev. 19:3). Are we to believe that cities, not merely people, are eternal and subject to the perpetual process of destruction, without ever really being destroyed? Clearly, the vision here is hyperbolic and intended to connect Babylon's complete destruction with the Old Testament story of God's wrath against Sodom and Gomorrah, which uses the same language and many of the same images (see Gen. 19:27–29; Isa. 34:10). In Genesis, Sodom and Gomorrah were utterly destroyed, but obviously they are not still burning today.

Third, throughout the New Testament, the unrighteous are condemned to separation from God. Jesus says that he will tell the wicked at the judgment, "I never knew you. Away from me, you evildoers!" (Matt. 7:23). Indeed, even advocates of eternal torment describe hell as "complete separation from God."[1] But remarkably, that is *not* what we read in Revelation 14. There, the wicked are said to "be tormented with burning sulfur *in the presence of the holy angels and of the Lamb*" (v. 10). Advocates of the eternal torture view say this verse should not be read literally. But they argue that the very next verse, "the smoke of their torment will rise for ever and ever," *should* be read literally.

Traditionalists tend to take this cherry-picking approach a few chapters later as well, in Revelation 19 and 20. There we read about the beast, the false prophet, and the devil being thrown into a lake of fire, where "they will be tormented day and night for ever and ever" (20:10). John also writes that, along with God's enemies, "death and Hades were thrown into the lake of fire" (20:14). How precisely are death and Hades tormented day and night forever? Or for that matter, how is an intangible power like death thrown anywhere at all? It seems obvious that John is using highly symbolic, nonliteral imagery in this verse, and yet the very next verse (20:15) is where we read about people being thrown into the lake of fire, which the eternal torture advocates insist isn't symbolic at all. Once again, using these passages to justify the doctrine of eternal torture requires knowing precisely when to turn our metaphorical reading on and off.

All these interpretive problems are solved, however, when we stop trying to flip between literal and metaphorical readings of Revelation. The vivid descriptions of judgment in chapters 14, 19, and 20 all use well-known apocalyptic symbols and language. In other words, we must read Revelation as apocalyptic literature rather than as didactic prose. The message is that the judgment of those aligned against God will be certain, severe, and permanent. The Lord is warning his people, with the most graphic imagery possible, not to be seduced by the evil of the world's oppressive empires. After describing the judgment, John says, "This calls for patient endurance on the part of the people of God who keep his commands and remain faithful to Jesus" (14:12).

With hyperbolic and vivid language, Revelation paints a picture of God's wrath against the world's injustice. It does not offer a photographic description of hell. For example, the lake of fire is identified twice as "the second death" (20:14; 21:8). With this detail, we can begin to make sense of death and Hades being thrown into the lake of fire. It's an apocalyptic way of communicating what Paul also says—that Christ will defeat every enemy

REWARD AND PUNISHMENT

and that "the last enemy to be *destroyed* is death" (1 Cor. 15:26). The burning sulfur, smoke rising forever, and the lake of fire are all Old Testament images of utter destruction that John employs to poetically communicate the absolute victory of Christ over his enemies and the complete destruction of all evil, injustice, and oppression in his redeemed world.

 READ MORE: 1 Corinthians 15:20–28; Revelation 20:10–15

51 IF JESUS WAS SERIOUS . . . THEN HIS MISSION IS ACCOMPLISHED THROUGH JOY, NOT FEAR

FOR SOME CHRISTIANS, particularly those seeking to spread the faith, the eternal conscious torment (ECT) doctrine is seen as an essential part of their missionary equipment. The fear of existing forever in agonizing pain has been wielded for centuries as an evangelistic tool. For many, the mere mention of the word "evangelism" brings to mind street preachers with megaphones and placards warning about the eternal flames that await the unrepentant. Traveling revivalists have been known to use fire-and-brimstone sermons to frighten unbelievers and wayward Christians into the fold.

Therefore, questioning the biblical foundations of ECT threatens to rob the church of one of its most powerful missionary tools. Without it, some fear the church will be less equipped to accomplish its mission. Defenders of ECT say that removing the traditional view of hell as eternal torment will make the church's mission much more difficult. It will diminish the urgency Christians feel to engage that mission, and it won't be as easy to win converts who are eager to escape eternity in hell.

As both politics and the advertising industry have shown, fear is a very effective motivator. It targets our most basic animal instinct for self-preservation, which resides in the least rational part of our brains. It's a proven biological and sociological fact that people respond to fear. And those who employ fear to lead or manipulate others feel powerful and effective. Therefore, we shouldn't be surprised that some Christians are extremely reluctant to abandon a fear-based approach to God's mission. And nothing is more frightening than the doctrine of ECT.

Rather than asking whether the traditional view of hell is *effective*, we ought to be asking whether it is *biblical*. As I noted in chapter 39, in Acts, when the apostles first proclaim the gospel and see thousands come to faith, hell is never mentioned. Not once. And fear is never the primary tactic used to persuade nonbelievers to give their allegiance to Christ.

This reality is not the case for much of popular American Christianity. When Karl Barth, the famed Swiss theologian, visited the United States, he was shocked by the evangelistic strategies he witnessed. "That was not the Good News," Barth said in response to an evangelist's sermon. "That was pistol-shooting. An urgent appeal was made to the people: You must, you should! . . . He wanted to scare people. To threaten always makes an impression. People would always much rather be frightened than be made joyful." Later, commenting on the American approach to Christ's mission, Barth said, "Christian faith begins with joy and not with fear."[1]

The wide gap between how the earliest Christians pursued their mission and how so many prefer to pursue it today is both revealing and troubling. Maybe the reason some are so eager to defend a frightening and unbiblical doctrine of eternal torture is that they don't know how to construct a joyful and biblical vision of Jesus. And that may also explain why so many Christians avoid talking about God's justice. They've believed a narrow caricature that equates biblical justice with nothing more than wrath and hell and have missed the larger vision of God's justice as restorative and benevolent. How different would the church's mission be if we stopped trying to motivate with a vision of fear and instead tried to inspire with a vision of redemptive justice?

WHAT IF JESUS WAS SERIOUS ABOUT JUSTICE?

As we've discovered, far from threatening or being unappealing, a proper understanding of God's justice is exactly what so much of our world longs to see. His justice defends the oppressed and rescues the enslaved. His justice is fierce yet full of mercy. Divine justice is incorruptible, making no distinction between the weak and the powerful. It transcends every boundary, uniting even the heavens and the earth. Through Christ, true justice has been perfectly revealed in the cross. Christ has defeated the power of evil, has reconciled us to God, and invites us to participate in his victory as we draw closer to the day when every wrong is made forever right.

 READ MORE: Acts 10:34–43; Revelation 22:1–5

NOTES

Introduction

1. Glenn Beck, quoted in Tobin Grant, "Glenn Beck: 'Leave Your Church,'" *Christianity Today*, March 12, 2010, https://www.christianitytoday.com/news/2010/march/20-51.0.html.

2. *First Greek Life of Pachomius* 4–5, in *The Life and Teaching of Pachomius*, Wellsprings of Faith 13 (Leominster, UK: Gracewing, 1998), 3.

3. For more on the origin and impact of dispensational theology in the United States, see Daniel G. Hummel, *The Rise and Fall of Dispensationalism: How the Evangelical Battle over the End Times Shaped a Nation* (Grand Rapids: Eerdmans, 2023); and Robert P. Jones, *White Too Long: The Legacy of White Supremacy in American Christianity* (New York: Simon & Schuster, 2020).

4. John R. W. Stott, *The Message of the Sermon on the Mount*, The Bible Speaks Today (Downers Grove, IL: InterVarsity, 1978), 67.

5. This section does not comprise a comprehensive discussion of the afterlife or heaven. For that, I recommend my previous book in this series, *What If Jesus Was Serious about Heaven? A Visual Guide to Experiencing God's Kingdom among Us* (Grand Rapids: Brazos, 2023).

Chapter 1 Then Our Understanding of Justice Must Begin in the Old Testament

1. Timothy Keller, *Generous Justice: How God's Grace Makes Us Just* (New York: Dutton, 2010), 4.

Chapter 2 Then Justice Is Part of God's Creation

1. John H. Walton, *The Lost World of Genesis One: Ancient Cosmology and the Origins Debate* (Downers Grove, IL: IVP Academic, 2009), 33.

Chapter 3 Then All People Are Made in God's Image and Crave Justice

1. C. S. Lewis, *Mere Christianity* (1952; repr., New York: HarperCollins, 2001), 6.

NOTES

Chapter 5 Then We Should Resist Evil

1. Quoted in Clayborne Carson and Peter Holloran, eds., *A Knock at Midnight: Inspiration from the Great Sermons of Reverend Martin Luther King, Jr.* (New York: Grand Central, 2001), 97.

2. The phrase is a summary of Dallas Willard's message. See John Ortberg's "Offer Gentle Noncooperation with Evil | John Ortberg," YouTube video, 11:53, posted by Become New on October 21, 2021, https://youtu.be/kmkdZVLtMW0. For more, see Dallas Willard, *The Spirit of the Disciplines: Understanding How God Changes Lives* (New York: HarperSanFrancisco, 1990), 229–30.

Chapter 10 Then Rest Is How We Remember and Extend Justice

1. Giorgia Silani, Claus Lamm, Christian C. Ruff, and Tania Singer, "Right Supramarginal Gyrus Is Crucial to Overcome Emotional Egocentricity Bias in Social Judgments," *Journal of Neuroscience* 33 (September 25, 2013): 15475.

Chapter 11 Then Just Laws Will Lead to Community Flourishing

1. The Sermon on the Mount is found in Matthew 5–7, and it's the focus of my first book in this series, *What If Jesus Was Serious? A Visual Guide to the Teachings of Jesus We Love to Ignore* (Chicago: Moody, 2020).

2. N. T. Wright, *Matthew for Everyone, Part 1: Chapters 1–15* (Louisville: Westminster John Knox, 2002), 80.

Chapter 13 Then Our Worship of God Will Be Multidimensional

1. Skye Jethani and David French, "French Friday: Falwell and the Fruit of Evangelical Leadership," *Holy Post Podcast*, January 28, 2022, https://www.holypost.com/post/french-friday-falwell-the-fruit-of-evangelical-leadership.

Chapter 14 Then Justice Is Essential to Worship

1. Mark Labberton, *The Dangerous Act of Worship: Living God's Call to Justice* (Downers Grove, IL: IVP Books, 2007), 37–38.

Chapter 15 Then True Worship Lifts Up Christ by Lifting Up the Oppressed

1. Rick Warren, *The Purpose Driven Church* (Grand Rapids: Zondervan, 1995), 280.

Chapter 19 Then Justice Is about Our Identity, Not the Other Person's

1. Elie Wiesel, quoted in Eugene H. Peterson, *Tell It Slant: A Conversation on the Language of Jesus in His Stories and Prayers* (Grand Rapids: Eerdmans, 2008), 38.

Chapter 22 Then Our Mercy, like God's, Should Exceed All Expectations

1. Most English translations of Exod. 34:7 add the word "generation" or "generations," which does not appear in the original Hebrew. Most Bibles say something like "he punishes the children and their children for the sin of the parents to the third and fourth *generation*." While this addition is not completely unjustified, it does obscure the poetic cadence of the original Hebrew. "Third and fourth" is supposed to stand in contrast to "thousands." This is not clear when "generation" is added.

Chapter 23 Then Justice Alone Won't Rescue Us from Our Sins

1. Gary M. Burge, *Jesus, the Middle Eastern Storyteller* (Grand Rapids: Zondervan, 2009), 87.

Chapter 25 Then We Will Be Judged by a Higher Standard Than the Golden Rule

1. Quoted in Michael Sharp, *The Book of Life: Ascension and the Divine World Order* (Brookline, MA: Avatar, 2004), 50.

Chapter 26 Then God Is Wrathful Because He Is Loving

1. "Statement 20: Hell Is a Real Place Where Certain People Will Be Punished Forever," The State of Theology, an outreach of Ligonier Ministries, https://thestateoftheology.com/data-explorer/2022/20.

2. Miroslav Volf, *Free of Charge: Giving and Forgiving in a Culture Stripped of Grace* (Grand Rapids: Zondervan, 2009), 138–39.

Chapter 27 Then God's Wrath Is Usually Passive, Not Active

1. John R. W. Stott, *The Cross of Christ* (Leicester, UK: Inter-Varsity, 1986), 173.

2. Abraham Lincoln, Second Inaugural Address, Washington, DC, March 4, 1865, transcription available at https://www.nps.gov/linc/learn/historyculture/lincoln-second-inaugural.htm (slightly modified).

Chapter 29 Then Empathy Heals Arrogance and Judgmentalism

1. Diane E. Dreher, "Why Do We Have an Empathy Deficit?," *Psychology Today*, November 13, 2017, https://www.psychologytoday.com/ie/blog/your-personal-renaissance/201711/why-do-we-have-empathy-deficit.

2. Mark Honigsbaum, "Barack Obama and the 'Empathy Deficit,'" *The Guardian*, January 4, 2013, https://www.theguardian.com/science/2013/jan/04/barack-obama-empathy-deficit.

3. Rasmus Hougaard and Jacqueline Carter, "Why Your Constant State of Busyness Is Bad for Your Health," *Fast Company*, January 14, 2022, https://www.fastcompany.com/90712204/why-your-constant-state-of-busyness-is-bad-for-your-health.

NOTES

4. Daisy Grewal, "How Wealth Reduces Compassion," *Scientific American*, April 10, 2012, https://www.scientificamerican.com/article/how-wealth-reduces-compassion.

5. See Bill Bishop, *The Big Sort: Why the Clustering of Like-Minded America Is Tearing Us Apart* (Evanston, IL: Houghton Mifflin, 2008).

Chapter 30 Then We Can't Reduce People to a Single Story or Sin

1. Bryan Stevenson, *Just Mercy: A Story of Justice and Redemption* (New York: Random House, 2014), 17.

2. See David Brooks, "In Praise of Equipoise," *New York Times*, September 1, 2017, https://www.nytimes.com/2017/09/01/opinion/in-praise-of-equipoise.html.

Chapter 31 Then the Cross Has Cosmic Implications

1. N. T. Wright, *Evil and the Justice of God* (Downers Grove, IL: IVP Books, 2006), 92.

Chapter 32 Then Jesus's Cross Is Bad News before It Is Good News

1. James D. Miller, *Looking at the Cross*, Being Reformed: Faith Seeking Understanding (Louisville: Congregational Ministries, Presbyterian Church USA, 2012), 8–9.

2. This account of G. K. Chesterton's short essay in *The Times* of London has been retold in many places. However, we lack documentary proof that Chesterton ever wrote the essay or that it was ever published in *The Times*.

3. Quoted in Dale W. Brown, *The Book of Buechner: A Journey through His Writings* (Louisville: Westminster John Knox, 2006), xvi.

Chapter 33 Then the Ugliness of the Cross Reveals God's Goodness

1. Fleming Rutledge, *The Crucifixion: Understanding the Death of Christ* (Grand Rapids: Eerdmans, 2015), 38.

2. Miroslav Volf, *Exclusion and Embrace: A Theological Exploration of Identity, Otherness, and Reconciliation* (Nashville: Abingdon, 1996), 298.

3. Dietrich Bonhoeffer, *The Cost of Discipleship*, trans. R. H. Fuller (London: SCM, 2015), 4.

4. Bonhoeffer, *Cost of Discipleship*, 4.

5. Volf, *Exclusion and Embrace*, 297.

Chapter 35 Then the Cross Is Primarily about God's Love

1. Many scholars believe that penal substitutionary atonement was first articulated by Anselm in the eleventh century and later expanded upon by Reformers like Martin Luther and John Calvin. But the early Christians and church fathers did not hold a penal substitutionary view of the cross.

NOTES

2. Steve Chalke and Alan Mann, *The Lost Message of Jesus* (Grand Rapids: Zondervan, 2004), 182.

3. For a discussion of the difference between active and passive wrath, see chap. 27.

4. N. T. Wright, *The Day the Revolution Began: Reconsidering the Meaning of Jesus's Crucifixion* (New York: HarperCollins, 2016), 147.

5. Augustine, *The Trinity 2*, trans. Edmund Hill (Hyde Park, NY: New City, 1991), 99.

6. Gregory of Nyssa, *On the Difference between Essence and Hypostasis*, quoted in Kallistos Ware, *The Orthodox Way* (Crestwood, NY: St. Vladimir's Seminary Press, 1979), 31.

Chapter 36 Then He Did Not Think of Me "Above All"

1. "Above All" is a Christian contemporary song cowritten by Paul Baloche and Lenny LeBlanc in 1995.

2. James D. Bratt, ed., *Abraham Kuyper: A Centennial Reader* (Grand Rapids: Eerdmans, 1998), 461.

Chapter 37 Then His Resurrection Did More Than Prove His Divine Identity

1. N. T. Wright, *Evil and the Justice of God* (Downers Grove, IL: IVP Books, 2006), 92.

Chapter 38 Then the Power of the Cross Is Still Working Today

1. Andrew Young, *An Easy Burden: The Civil Rights Movement and the Transformation of America* (New York: HarperCollins, 1996), 223.

Chapter 39 Then God's Judgment Is Not the Same as Hell

1. Skye Jethani, *What If Jesus Was Serious about Heaven? A Visual Guide to Experiencing God's Kingdom among Us* (Grand Rapids: Brazos, 2023).

2. Some translations refer to "Hades" in Peter's sermon on Pentecost (Acts 2:27, 31). In the New Testament, the Greek word *hadēs* was a generic term for the grave or the realm of the dead. It is not synonymous with "hell" (Greek *gehenna*), which Jesus used to describe a place of punishment and destruction.

Chapter 40 Then Not Everyone Will Experience Eternal Life with God

1. C. S. Lewis, *The Problem of Pain* (1940; repr., New York: HarperOne, 2009), 118.

2. See Robert Herguth, "Top Lutheran Bishop: If Hell Exists, 'I Think It's Empty,'" *Chicago Sun-Times*, March 7, 2018, https://chicago.suntimes.com/2018/3/7/18372814/top-lutheran-bishop-if-hell-exists-i-think-it-s-empty.

3. Lewis, *Problem of Pain*, 127.

NOTES

Chapter 41 Then Not Everyone Will Receive the Same Reward or Punishment

1. Jonathan Edwards, *The Works of Jonathan Edwards*, vol. 2–3 (Woodstock, Ontario: Devoted, 2017), 342.
2. Edwards, *Works of Jonathan Edwards*, 342.

Chapter 42 Then Hell Isn't Just a Place on Earth

1. Martyrdom and Ascension of Isaiah 4:14, 18, quoted in Gerbern S. Oegema, *The Anointed and His People: Messianic Expectations from the Maccabees to Bar Kochba*, Journal for the Study of the Pseudepigrapha Supplement Series 27 (Sheffield: Sheffield Academic, 1998), 241.

Chapter 43 Then God's Justice Is Undying, but Those Who Face It Are Not

1. Denny Burk, "Eternal Conscious Torment," in *Four Views on Hell*, ed. Preston Sprinkle, 2nd ed. (Grand Rapids: Zondervan, 2016), 23 (emphasis added).

Chapter 44 Then Not Every Human Soul Is Immortal

1. Tertullian, *On the Resurrection of the Soul* 3, in *The Ante-Nicene Fathers: Translations of the Writings of the Fathers down to A.D. 325*, ed. Alexander Roberts and James Donaldson, 10 vols. (1885–87; repr., Peabody, MA: Hendrickson, 1994), 3:547.
2. Le Roy Edwin Froom, *The Conditionalist Faith of Our Fathers* (Washington, DC: Review & Herald, 1965), 1:951.

Chapter 46 Then Finite Sins Cannot Be Punished with Infinite Torture

1. Denny Burk, "Eternal Conscious Torment," in *Four Views on Hell*, ed. Preston Sprinkle, 2nd ed. (Grand Rapids: Zondervan, 2016), 20.

Chapter 48 Then the Wicked Will Face Death and Will Pay for Their Sins

1. Pseudo-Philo 16.3, quoted in Daniel M. Gurtner, ed., *This World and the World to Come: Soteriology in Early Judaism*, Library of Second Temple Studies 74 (London: T&T Clark International, 2011), 53.
2. N. T. Wright, *Surprised by Hope: Rethinking Heaven, the Resurrection, and the Mission of the Church* (New York: HarperOne, 2008), 182.

Chapter 49 Then His Parable about Lazarus and the Rich Man Isn't about Hell

1. N. T. Wright, *Surprised by Hope: Rethinking Heaven, the Resurrection, and the Mission of the Church* (New York: HarperOne, 2008), 177.

Chapter 50 Then the Lake of Fire in Revelation Is about Destruction

1. This view finds biblical support from multiple texts, including 2 Thess. 1:9.

Chapter 51 Then His Mission Is Accomplished through Joy, Not Fear

1. Karl Barth, press conference, San Francisco, May 15, 1962, in Karl Barth, *Gespräche 1959–1962*, ed. Eberhard Busch (Alexandria, VA: Alexander Street, 2007), 525, cited in Christiane Tietz, *Karl Barth: A Life in Conflict* (Oxford: Oxford University Press, 2021), 385.